PRESERVING DIGITAL INFORMATION

A How-To-Do-It Manual

Gregory S. Hunter

**HOW-TO-DO-IT MANUALS
FOR LIBRARIANS**

NUMBER 93

NEAL-SCHUMAN PUBLISHERS, INC.
New York, London

Published by Neal-Schuman Publishers, Inc.
100 Varick Street
New York, NY 10013

Printed and bound in the United States of America.

ISBN 1–55570–353–4

Library of Congress Cataloging-in-Publication Data

Hunter, Gregory S.
    Preserving digital information : a how-to-do-it manual / Gregory S. Hunter.
       p.   cm. — (How-to-do-it manual ; no. 93)
    Includes bibliographical references.
    ISBN 1-55570-353-4 (alk. paper)
      1. Computer files—Conservation and restoration. 2. Computer files—Conservation and restoration—United States. I. Title. II. How-to-do-it manuals for librarians ; no. 93.

Z701.3.C65 H86 2000
025.8'4—dc 21
                                00-035147

To my wife, Joann.
May these words composed on a computer screen
Preserve into the future
The wonder of the love we share

CONTENTS

LIST OF FIGURES

LIST OF TABLES

PREFACE

Both of my teenage daughters share an interest in the performing arts. Beth, a high school junior, is an aspiring musician; Kate, a seventh grader, is a singer and stage performer. On reflection, my daughters' interests in live performance are not all that different from my own interests in preserving digital information.

Consider a live jazz session performance. How can you "preserve" a jazz performance? Can this dynamic reality be "fixed" in time? Is preservation a futile exercise? After all, the next time the song is performed it will, by definition, be completely different. Who decides which jazz performances will be preserved and what criteria do they use in making a selection?

Or consider a play performed night after night. Each performance is a little different from every other one. Should there be a "record" of the production? If so, would we preserve one entire performance or an assemblage of the best moments of several performances? Would the latter be an "authentic record"?

I see many parallels to the world of digital information. Whether we are dealing with a local database or the World Wide Web, how do we determine if "records" exist? What strategies can we use to capture and preserve the information we think should be retained? Will this information really survive for the long term? In brief, is our present digital world as fleeting as a jazz performance or as mutable as a theatrical run?

These are some of the issues I address in *Preserving Digital Information: A How-To-Do-It Manual*. It is the best and worst of times for preserving digital information. It is the best of times because so much important work has been accomplished in the last few years; the worst of times because information technologies develop and expand at ever faster rates. I tried to convey both the excitement leading researchers feel and the uncertainty of front-line practitioners. We seek incremental solutions and develop best practices through the shared power of the Internet.

Preserving Digital Information is a practical guide to digital preservation—a state changing rapidly and without warning. I discuss the preservation of information created in digital form as well as items converted from analog to digital representations. I include the theoretical underpinnings which will serve the reader well in making decisions in this swiftly changing field. In addition, I offer best practices from a variety of institutional settings.

Whether this is your first effort at digital preservation or simply the next step in a long experience with preserving digital records, archivists and preservation administrators will find *Preserving Digital Information* a useful guide. Librarians will discover the needed guidance to work effectively with archivists and preservation officers planning for the safekeeping of this rapidly changing medium. Anyone working with digital records of any kind—at home, in an office, or in a library—will find a systematic explanation of the difficulties that such records present and some very practical recommendations for meeting the challenges.

Preserving Digital Information is divided into seven chapters.

Chapter 1 is an overview of digital information and the preservation challenges we face.

Chapter 2 covers the nature of digital information, especially methods of representation and options for physical media.

Chapter 3 summarizes the approaches and major findings of eight influential research initiatives on digital preservation and electronic records. Each of these projects is helping to shape solutions to the challenges of digital preservation.

Chapter 4 reviews a number of storage, handling, and preservation best practices. This chapter gives specific advice on the best storage environment and the proper way to handle the physical media.

Chapter 5 addresses the specific preservation challenges that two types of digital information pose: electronic mail and Web pages. E-mail and the World Wide Web are changing the way organizations do business, and it is likely that they will also force us to reassess the way we preserve information, even other digital information.

Chapter 6 relates digital imaging to the preservation program, relying heavily upon research conducted at major research libraries. Imaging, or scanning, reformats analog materials from paper or microfilm and is often an institution's entrée into the world of digital preservation.

Chapter 7 presents an integrated approach to the preservation of information in larger systems rather than simply the preservation of individual digital documents. Here is a discussion of assumptions and strategic decisions, as well as a multi-step approach to implementing a digital preservation program. I see it as a roadmap for the archivist or preservation administrator. An extensive list of sources for further information, both in electronic and paper form, completes this guide.

I have presented the basic concepts of digital preservation systematically and most people will find reading *Preserving Digital Information* from beginning to end helpful. However, those with more extensive knowledge of the nature of digital records may prefer to read only those parts of the theoretical background with which they are less familiar or go directly to the practical recommendations. The detailed table of contents makes it possible to approach the topic in many ways.

There are numerous strategies for dealing with this multi-faceted information, and just as the digital formats are in a state of constant change, so are there always new strategies for dealing with the preservation issues that this state of flux presents. *Preserving Digital Information* demystifies some of these ever-changing formats and furnishes step-by-step plans for making the best possible decisions to ensure today's digital information remains available tomorrow.

ACKNOWLEDGMENTS

I have many people to thank for assistance with this book, though, of course, responsibility for the final product is my own. In particular, several consulting projects dealing with electronic records and digital preservation enabled me to clarify and refine my thinking on these topics. I am indebted to Mary Hedge and Lauren Barnes of American Express; Elizabeth Adkins and Susan Field of Ford Motor Company; Jim Berberich and Gerard Clark of the Florida Bureau of Archives and Records Management; Bill Ptacek and Cathy Danahy of the Nebraska Division of Records Management; and Frank Suran and Linda Avetta of the Pennsylvania Historical and Museum Commission.

In terms of this manuscript, my thanks go to Paul Conway of Yale University for his critical reading of an earlier draft and his helpful comments. My editor at Neal-Schuman, Charles Harmon, has been a model of patience, persistence, and professionalism throughout the project, my second with this publisher. Pat Schuman has been a friend since we served together on a grants review panel in the 1970s and as adjunct faculty members at Columbia University in the 1980s.

Finally, I cannot thank my family enough—my wife, Joann, and my daughters, Beth and Kate—for their support and understanding. The countless hours spent with my laptop computer were at the expense of time with them that I treasure so much. I look forward to more time together, sharing music and live theater—with or without the comparisons to digital information.

Gregory S. Hunter
June 2000

1 DIGITAL INFORMATION: THE PRESERVATION CHALLENGE

As the year 2000 approached, the *New York Times* decided to mark the occasion in a special way. The *Times* involved its staff and outside experts in creating "a time capsule filled with artifacts to give people living in the year 3000 some idea of who we were and how we lived."[1]

The *Times* included a variety of items, from the serious to the whimsical. Examples of the former included a "field guide" to plants and animals that will be extinct by the year 3000 and an "encyclopedia of lost practices" to document some of our cherished habits and diversions. Among the whimsical was a David Letterman list, "The Top 10 Things People in the Year 3000 Should Know about Us," that included the following items: "Y2K—We were on top of it. Y3K—you're on your own." "If you wanted a billion dollars, all you had to do was think of a word and add dot com."[2]

As the *Times* planned a time capsule, it wanted to make certain that the capsule would last for 1,000 years. Therefore, the editors assembled a group of experts to talk about the practical issues involved in building a time capsule. The editor of the *Times* began the luncheon discussion with the following comments: "We're not that interested in a conventional time capsule. A box full of stuff buried in a hole seems old-fashioned. We're leaning instead toward some sort of digital capsule. What do you think?"[3]

Five hours later, the luncheon conversation was still under way. The experts proceeded to give the editors a primer on the challenges of digital preservation. Point by point, the panel members showed why digital data, sealed in a capsule, were unlikely to be readable in 1,000 years. To the surprise of the *Times,* the experts extolled the preservation value of analog over digital. Among the points they made were:

- "Digital is a problem. Digital storage media—floppies, compact discs, whatever—don't have a long life span. A few decades at most."
- "Digital storage is an all-or-nothing proposition. Once the zeroes and ones that make up the digital record start to break down, the entire disc or tape becomes unreadable. Analog is different. When an old photo deteriorates, you can still see some of it. But when a digital image deteriorates, you lose the whole ball of wax."
- "Reading a digital record requires electronic translation of the

"The advent of electronic information introduces new preservation requirements. In contrast with print materials, where to preserve the artifact is to preserve the information contained in it, electronic information is easily transferred from one medium to another with no loss."—Peter S. Graham, *Intellectual Preservation: Electronic Preservation of the Third Kind.*

zeroes and ones into text or pictures or sound. If you don't have the right hardware or software, you're out of luck. This happens now after a couple of years. Some of NASA's early images of the earth are no longer readable. We've been using the equipment in a state of faith, not fact. In 1,000 years, who will understand such strange, ephemeral technology? It's already hard enough to find a disk drive for 5 1/4-inch floppies."

- "Right now, your only option is to 'migrate' the digital data—keep copying it over onto the latest format. But that's a lot of work. Besides, the whole point of a time capsule is that people aren't supposed to be able to see what's in there."

"Information technology is revolutionizing our concept of record keeping in an upheaval as great as the introduction of printing, if not of writing itself. The current generation of digital records has unique historical significance. Yet these documents are far more fragile than paper, placing the chronicle of our entire period in jeopardy."—Jeff Rothenberg, "Ensuring the Longevity of Digital Documents."

The experts assembled by the *Times* identified some of the major challenges in preserving digital information: fragile physical media, silent deterioration, hardware and software dependence, and the need to copy data regularly.

Do these challenges mean that we should abandon digital preservation completely? Even if such a course of action were possible in the short run, it would become increasingly difficult in the future as more and more items are "born digital" and never even exist in analog form. Like it or not, the digital domain will have to include a preservation component.

Preserving Digital Information is a practical guide to this preservation component according to the technology available at the beginning of the 21st century. To begin the discussion, let's look in a little more depth at the three words contained in the title of the book: *Preserving Digital Information*.

PRESERVING

Preservation encompasses a wide variety of interrelated activities designed to prolong the usable life of books, archives, manuscripts, and artifacts. It is a broad term that covers protection, stabilization, and treatment of documents. Preservation is one of the three core functions of the archivist, the other two being identification and use.

According to Paul Conway, "At one time, advocates for the protection of cultural artifacts, including books, primary source documents, and museum objects, used the terms 'conservation' and 'preservation' interchangeably. Today, preservation is an umbrella term for the many policies and options for action, including conservation treatments. Preservation is the acquisition, organization, and distribution of resources to prevent further deterioration or renew the usability of selected groups of materials."[4]

Most preservation programs take a phased approach that emphasizes broad stabilizing actions to protect the entire holdings of a repository rather than the concentration of resources solely on item-level treatment. Such an approach includes

- understanding the nature of the preservation problem;
- conducting preservation surveys to establish priorities;
- controlling the storage environment;
- planning for disasters;
- performing holdings maintenance;
- treating selected materials.[5]

Most of these activities are also appropriate for the digital environment.

"Preservation management encompasses all the policies, procedures, and processes that together prevent further deterioration of physical objects, renew the information they contain, and increase their functional value."—Paul Conway, *Preservation in the Digital World.*

DIGITAL

As will be discussed in Chapter 2, *digital* means that there are discrete states with no other choices, like the seconds on a digital watch. A digital device will "jump" from one value to another without crossing all the values in between. In contrast, *analog* means that something varies continuously, like a wristwatch with a sweep second hand. In terms of computers, digital usually is combined with *binary*, the use of two discrete states.

Very often the term *digital* is used interchangeably with *electronic*, as when archivists talk about managing "electronic records." In reality, the two terms have quite different meanings. As the name implies, electronic refers to something produced by the action of electrons, specifically in an electrical current (which is nothing more than a stream of moving electrons).

Digital information can be represented in nonelectronic form, using optical or quantum techniques. Likewise, electronic information need not necessarily be digital.[6] For example, the VHS movies that we watch at home are electronic, meaning they were produced by the action of electrons. However, they are not digital because the images vary continuously rather than having discrete states. To avoid confusion, throughout this book I use the term *digital information* rather than *electronic information*.

INFORMATION

Information is another word that is used and misused. One author calls it "data repackaged in a meaningful form."[7] I prefer to think of information as one point on a progression from data to archives:

- *Data:* The content or "facts" that we wish to process
- *Information*: The data communicated or received
- *Document*: The information in context
- *Record*: The document preserved
- *Archives*: A record preserved for its enduring value

Thinking of information as part of a continuum also illustrates the increasing complexity of the preservation challenge. Preserving anything beyond data means that we also have to preserve other things: the communication of the information, the context of the document, the integrity of the record, and the value of the archives. If all we had to do was preserve the data or content, our task would be much simpler.

Where does this preservation of digital information take place? Is it in a digital *archives*[8] or a digital *library*? Are these two separate types of repositories or are they really one and the same? As defined by a joint task force of the Research Libraries Group and the Commission on Preservation and Access, these two repositories have related but distinct missions:

- *Digital archives* are responsible for ensuring the integrity and long-term accessibility of our cultural heritage in digital form.
- *Digital libraries* collect and provide access to digital information but may or may not provide for the long-term storage of that information.

In the short run, digital archives tend to overlap the functions of a digital library. Not all digital libraries, however, provide the preservation function of a digital archives.[9] Because of the long-term nature of digital preservation, this book will focus more on the digital archives than the digital library.

THE PRESERVATION CHALLENGE

During the last two decades, archivists and preservation administrators have become more aware of the challenges posed by digital information. They also have tried to define the ways in which digital preservation is the same as or different from the preservation of information on other media.

Peter S. Graham has defined three different aspects of digital preservation:

- *Medium preservation*: The preservation of the physical media on which the bits and bytes of electronic information reside.
- *Technology preservation*: Refreshing of technologies from old to new as they become available.
- *Intellectual preservation*: Addressing the integrity and authenticity of the information as originally recorded. This involves strategies for dealing with three kinds of changes: accidental change, intentional change that is well meant, and intentional change that is not well meant (fraud).[10]

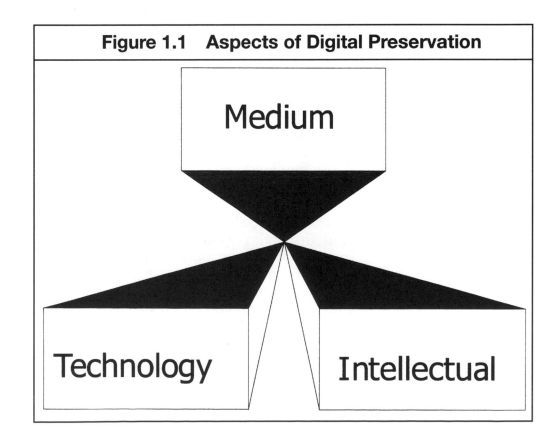

Figure 1.1   Aspects of Digital Preservation

Intellectual preservation is, perhaps, the most unfamiliar area. With information on paper, the authenticity and integrity of the information, once established at the time of transfer, is seldom changed in the course of preservation custody. Digital records require much more diligence on this score.

In the words of Jeff Rothenberg, digital documents require more diligence because they possess a "unique collection of core digital attributes" that must be retained. These attributes include the ability to be

- copied perfectly;
- accessed without geographic constraint;
- disseminated at virtually no incremental cost;
- machine-readable in all phases of their creation and distribution.

In addition, documents that are "born digital" tend to be dynamic, hyperlinked, and interactive—additional attributes that may need to be preserved.[11] Our experience preserving information on paper has not provided adequate strategies for preserving these core digital attributes.

A first step in developing a strategy is to realize the goals of that strategy. Paul Conway has stated these goals as follows:

- *Make use possible.* For some badly deteriorated items, digital copies may be the only way to provide access to the content of the records.
- *Protect original items.* After digitization, the original can be removed from use, thereby promoting its preservation.
- *Maintain digital objects.* Once captured in digital form, maintaining the digital representation becomes the preservation focus.[12]

Developing a framework for the preservation focus has been a priority for archivists and librarians during the 1990s. There have been several attempts at developing a framework, the most influential of which resulted from a task force established by the Commission on Preservation and Access, and the Research Libraries Group. The next section discusses this report in detail.[13]

A FRAMEWORK FOR DIGITAL PRESERVATION

In 1996, John Garrett of CyberVillages Corporation and Donald Waters of Yale University served as cochairs of a Task Force on Archiving of Digital Information. The task force was composed of representatives from industry, museums, archives, libraries, publishers, scholarly societies, and government. The Commission on Preservation and Access and the Research Libraries Group charged the task force to

- frame the key problems (organizational, technological, legal, economic, etc.) that need to be resolved;
- define the critical issues that inhibit resolution of each identified problem;
- recommend actions to remove each issue from the list;
- consider alternatives to technology refreshing;
- make other recommendations, as appropriate.

The task force report began with a very succinct statement of the challenge of archiving digital information. According to the task force, as hardware and software environments change with increasing rapidity, technological obsolescence has become a bigger problem than media fragility. In response to this challenge, archivists adopted the technique of "refreshing" digital media by copying information onto new media. As discussed in Chapter 4, refreshing eventually proved to be an incomplete solution and gave way to such strategies as migration and emulation.[14]

Legal and organizational issues also present challenges to a digital preservation initiative. As case law continues to evolve, questions remain about intellectual property (trademarks and copyrights) in the digital environment. Our *organizations* also must evolve because of the complex financial considerations and structural factors involved in a commitment to digital preservation. We need to build a deep infrastructure almost from scratch. This infrastructure will provide the systemic supports enabling us to "tame anxieties and move our cultural records naturally and confidently into the future."[15]

Moving these cultural records into the future requires an awareness of the *integrity* of digital information. According to the task force, our central goal must be to preserve information integrity—those features of an "information object" that distinguish it as "a whole and singular work." In the digital world, there are five features that determine information integrity: content, fixity, reference, provenance, and context.[16]

"Public debate about digital data preservation often focuses on how well the recording media themselves—magnetic tape, CD-ROMs, etc.—will stand up to age and physical wear, but archivists say technical obsolescence is a far bigger concern."—Leslie J. Nicholson, "The Post-Y2K Bug: Technical Obsolescence."

1. *Content.* Content is the intellectual substance found in information objects. This intellectual substance, however, operates at several levels of abstraction. At the lowest level is a simple bitstream of 1s (ones) and 0s (zeros). At a higher level, content depends on the structure and format of the representation (for example, as a word-processing file). Ultimately, content is defined by the knowledge or ideas that the digital object contains.

2. *Fixity.* For a digital object to have integrity, its content must be fixed as a discrete object. If an object is subject to change without notice, then its integrity may be compromised and its value as a cultural record diminished. Digital records are particularly subject to change because of their dynamic nature. Several techniques exist for establishing fixity, many of which involve cryptography or digital "signatures."

3. *Reference.* Information objects must have a consistent means of reference. For an object to maintain its integrity, one must be able to locate it definitively and reliably among other objects over time. For books and other analog objects, there are long-established systems of citation, description, and classification. While these are being adapted to the digital environment, universal solutions are not yet in place. One need only try to access a series of Internet addresses from several years ago to demonstrate how inconsistent our digital references can be.

4. *Provenance.* Provenance is one of the key principles of archival science. Provenance means that the integrity of an information object is partly embedded in tracing its source. Preserving provenance means that a digital archives must preserve a record of the origin and chain of custody of the information object. This helps to create a presumption that an object is authentic, that it is what it purports to be, and that its content has not been manipulated, altered, or falsified.

5. *Context.* Context refers to the ways in which a digital object interacts with elements in the wider digital environment. The context includes a technical dimension (hardware and software dependencies); a dimension of linkage to other objects (such as hyperlinks on the World Wide Web); a communications dimension (such as distribution on a network); and a wider social dimension (political and organizational considerations).

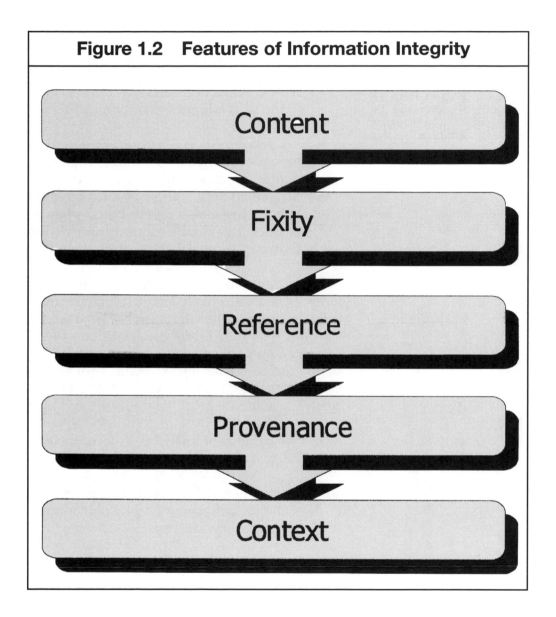

Figure 1.2 Features of Information Integrity

Turning from the challenge of digital information, the task force report concluded by discussing several infrastructure issues: stakeholder interests, archival roles and responsibilities, migration strategies, and cost modeling. These main points were made:

- "The first line of defense against the loss of valuable digital information rests with the creators, providers and owners of digital information."
- "Long-term preservation of digital information on a scale adequate for the demands of future research and scholarship will

"Preservation is access, and access is preservation."—Patricia Battin, writing in The Commission on Preservation and Access's Annual Report, 1992–1993.

require a deep infrastructure capable of supporting a distributed system of digital archives."

- "A critical component of the digital archiving infrastructure is the existence of a sufficient number of trusted organizations capable of storing, migrating and providing access to digital collections."
- "A process of certification for digital archives is needed to create an overall climate of trust about the prospects of preserving digital information."
- "Certified digital archives must have the right and duty to exercise an aggressive rescue function as a fail-safe mechanism for preserving valuable digital information that is in jeopardy of destruction, neglect or abandonment by its current custodian."[17]

In the time since this seminal task force report, organizations individually and collectively have explored strategies for building the "deep infrastructure." The latest effort was an announcement in March 2000 that the Research Libraries Group and the OCLC Online Computer Library Center have begun discussing ways the two organizations can cooperate to create infrastructures for digital archiving. The groups will collaborate on two working documents to establish best practices:

- "Attributes of a Digital Archive for Research Repositories"
- "Preservation Metadata for Long-Term Retention"

The two groups intend to bring key players together to review progress to date and identify common practices among those most experienced in the digital archiving area.[18]

CONCLUSION

The actual preservation strategy is the subject of the rest of this book. As will be seen, the growing realization of the preservation challenge has, in fact, spawned numerous strategies, some tested and others not yet tested. This should not be surprising given the dynamic nature of the computing environment.

NOTES

1. *New York Times Magazine,* Special Issue, Section 6, December 5, 1999. The quote is from the front cover.
2. Niles Eldredge, "A Field Guide to the Sixth Extinction," *New York Times Magazine* 144+. "An Encyclopedia of Lost Practices" 148+. David Letterman, "A Top 10 List to Last," 212.
3. An article presenting excerpts from the discussion, "Built to Last," begins on page 84. The experts were: Mary Turner Baker, Research Chemist, Smithsonian Center for Materials Research and Education; Gregory Benford, Professor of Physics, University of California, Irvine; Ronald Garner, Manager, Westinghouse Government Technical Services Division; Margaret MacLean, Conservation Planner and Consultant; Dianne Van Der Reyden, Head of the Paper Conservation Laboratory, Smithsonian Center for Materials Research and Education; and Frederick Stumm, Project Chief, United States Geological Survey, Water Resources Division.
4. Paul Conway, *Preservation in the Digital World* (Washington, DC: Commission on Preservation and Access, 1996), 5.
5. This framework is taken from Lewis J. Bellardo and Lynn Lady Bellardo, *A Glossary for Archivists, Manuscript Curators, and Records Managers* (Chicago: Society of American Archivists, 1992). The best one-volume discussion of preservation for archivists is Mary Lynn Ritzenthaler, *Preserving Archives and Manuscripts* (Chicago: Society of American Archivists, 1993). See also Gregory S. Hunter, *Developing and Maintaining Practical Archives: A How-To-Do-It Manual* (New York: Neal-Schuman, 1997). Norvell M. M. Jones and Mary Lynn Ritzenthaler, "Implementing an Archival Preservation Program," in James Gregory Bradsher, ed., *Managing Archives and Archival Institutions* (Chicago: University of Chicago Press, 1989), 185–206.
6. Jeff Rothenberg, *Avoiding Technological Quicksand: Finding a Viable Technical Foundation for Digital Preservation* (Washington, DC: Council on Library and Information Resources, 1999), 3.
7. Kurt F. Laukner and Mildred D. Lintner, *The Computer Continuum* (Indianapolis: Que Education and Training, Macmillan, 1999), G-11.
8. In keeping with standard archival practice, I will use the term "archives" as a collective noun with an "s" always at the end. To further confuse the matter, "archives" can mean three different things: the records themselves, the location where the records are housed, and the agency responsible for the records program. See

Hunter, *Practical Archives,* Chapter 1. For an excellent treatment of the applicability of archives to the digital environment, see Anne J. Gilliland-Swetland, *Enduring Paradigm, New Opportunities: The Value of the Archival Perspective in the Digital Environment* (Washington, DC: Council on Library and Information Resources, 2000).

9. John Garrett and Donald Waters, *Preserving Digital Information: Report of the Task Force on Archiving of Digital Information* (Washington, DC: Commission on Preservation and Access and the Research Libraries Group, 1996), 8. Available at *www.rlg.org/ArchTF/*.

10. Peter S. Graham, "Long-Term Intellectual Preservation," in Nancy E. Elkington, ed., *Digital Imaging Technology for Preservation: Proceedings from an RLG Symposium Held March 17 and 18, 1994, Cornell University, Ithaca, New York* (Mountain View, CA: The Research Libraries Group, 1994), 41-44. Also see Graham's *Intellectual Preservation: Electronic Preservation of the Third Kind* (Washington, DC: Commission on Preservation and Access, 1994).

11. Rothenberg, *Avoiding Technological Quicksand,* 3.

12. Conway, *Preservation in the Digital World,* 12.

13. Garrett and Waters, *Preserving Digital Information.* For other frameworks and statements of research issues, see: National Historical Publications and Records Commission, *Research Issues in Electronic Records* (St. Paul, MN: Minnesota Historical Society, 1991); *Electronic Records Research and Development: Final Report of the 1996 Conference Held at the University of Michigan, Ann Arbor, June 28–29, 1996,* (Ann Arbor, MI: University of Michigan, 1997), available at *www.si.umich.edu/e-recs/*.

14. Migrating electronic records involves moving them from old systems to new, open systems. At this time the only way known to migrate the records and their essential software functionality is to write special purpose codes or programs. Emulation means that one computer system is made to act like another one, as when a personal computer emulates (acts like) a dumb terminal connected to a mainframe computer.

15. Garrett and Waters, *Preserving Digital Information,* 7.

16. Garrett and Waters, *Preserving Digital Information,* 11–19.

17. Garrett and Waters, *Preserving Digital Information,* 40.

18. "RLG and OCLC Explore Digital Archiving," press release dated March 10, 2000. A second potential part of the "deep infrastructure" also was publicized in March 2000. The U.S. National Archives and Records Administration has been working with the San Diego Supercomputer Center to define an approach for maintaining digital data for hundreds of years. The approach requires

developing an environment that "supports migration of collections onto new software systems." The solution must include scalable technology for managing media and context migration. For a report on work to date, see Reagan Moore, et al., "Collection-Based Persistent Digital Archives: Part 1," *D-Lib Magazine* 6:3 (March 2000), available at *www.dlib.org/dlib/march00/moore/03moore-pt1.html.*

2 THE NATURE OF DIGITAL INFORMATION

Before we can *preserve* digital information, we need to understand something about its *nature*, what makes it different from the world of paper that has dominated the last few hundred years. The difference involves two major aspects:

- Digital representation
- Physical media

DIGITAL REPRESENTATION

Modern information systems are based on digital principles: ones and zeros represent the presence or absence of a physical reality (like electrical current). What are the implications of this? Basically, any type of information we wish to store and manipulate with a computer—numbers, text, images, sounds, etc.—must be converted from analog to digital form.

"Analog" means that something varies continuously, like a wristwatch with a sweep second hand. In an analog world, we are able to say, "It's approximately a quarter after five," which means, "It's analogous to quarter after five." It is common to express an analog reality as a wave, a flowing continuum of choices.

In contrast, a digital world is one in which there are discrete states with no other choices. A digital watch shows either 5:15 or 5:16, but cannot be somewhere in the middle. Instead of a wave, which varies continuously, a digital representation is limited to specific, predefined choices. Translated into computer terms, digital means that something is either 1 or 0, yes or no, on or off.

These basic principles are at the heart of our representation[1] of the following:

- Numbers
- Text
- Images
- Sounds
- Instructions

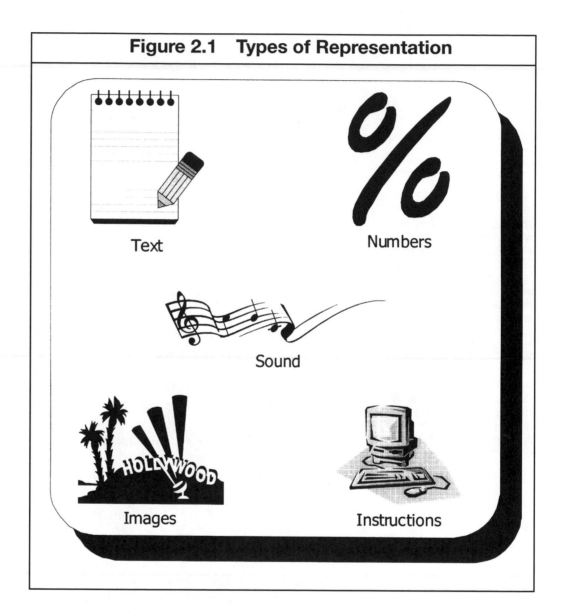

Figure 2.1 Types of Representation

Text

Numbers

Sound

Images

Instructions

REPRESENTING NUMBERS

We represent numbers all the time, without thinking about it. From our youngest days, we are taught to count using a particular system of representation: the decimal system. As the Latin root of the word implies, the decimal system uses 10 different symbols to represent reality (the numbers 0 through 9). This is why we call the decimal system base 10.

What happens when we have a number greater than 9? The decimal system adds placeholders to the left, as necessary, with each place increasing in value. In addition, the place values of each position are powers of ten.

Moving from right to left, the first four of these places are

Thousand $= 10 \times 10 \times 10 = 10^3$	Hundred $= 10 \times 10 = 10^2$	Ten $= 10 = 10^1$	One $= 10^0$ (anything raised to the "zero power" always equals 1)

We use the combination of ten distinct symbols and placeholders of increasing value to represent a number as follows:

Place Value	Thousand	Hundred	Ten	One
Discrete Symbol (0-9)	3	8	0	2
Calculation	3 x 1,000	8 x 100	0 x 10	2 x 1
Total	3,000	800	0	2

Therefore, the above number is 3,802.

We are so used to base 10 that we may think it the only way to represent numbers. However, we do have experiences with other bases. Take base 12, for instance. Have you ever ordered a dozen bagels or measured the number of inches in a foot? If so, you were using a system based on 12, but without 12 distinct characters.[2]

Representing numbers for a computer follows the same basic principle as the base 10 example above. In this case, however, we are translating the number into a binary code, base 2, in mathematics. Base two uses only two symbols, 0 and 1. Also, the place values of each position are powers of two.

Each base-2 placeholder represents one binary digit, or bit. Eight of these bits equal a byte. The value of each of these bits is as follows:

128	64	32	16	8	4	2	1
$= 2^7$	$= 2^6$	$= 2^5$	$= 2^4$	$= 2^3$	$= 2^2$	$= 2^1$	$= 2^0$

The way we would calculate a number is as follows:

Place Value	128	64	32	16	8	4	2	1
Discrete Symbol (0-1)	1	0	0	1	1	0	1	1
Calculation	1 x 128	0 x 64	0 x 32	1 x 16	1 x 8	0 x 4	1 x 2	1 x 1
Total	128	0	0	16	8	0	2	1

To summarize, the number "10011011" in base 2 equals 161 in base 10. If this were not confusing enough, the number 10011011 could also represent text, images, sound, or instructions, depending upon how the computer is programmed to interpret it. The next sections will discuss this further.

REPRESENTING TEXT

In order to represent text, we need two things:

- A defined universe, or *set*, of characters to represent. The set of characters must include not only letters and numbers, but punctuation marks and "control" characters, such as an end of paragraph mark.
- An agreed-upon symbol to represent each character in the set.

These requirements lead to the development of standards, since everyone must use the same characters and symbols if we are to communicate information. There must be a uniform code from one computer to the next. I will come back to standards several times in this volume, for the use of standards is one of the best ways of assuring the preservation of digital information.

Many computer codes have been created, but only two of these codes have become standards.

- IBM developed the Extended Binary Coded Decimal Interchange Code (EBCDIC) for use on large, mainframe computers.
- The American National Standards Institute (ANSI), the U.S. standard-setting organization, issued the American Standard Code for Information Interchange (ASCII). All personal computers use ASCII code for representing characters

ASCII originally had only 128 characters but has been extended to 256 characters. One would convert textual information into a computer representation in the following way:

"We continue to produce digital records in formats with short life spans that are increasingly difficult and sometimes impossible to access years later."—Rich Lysakowski and Zahava Leibowitz, *Titanic 2020: A Call to Action.*

1. Match each printed character with a character in the ASCII set
2. Record the associated number from the ASCII character set
3. Store these numbers in binary form in the computer's memory

For example, this is how one would convert the word cat into something the computer can understand:

Text Character	c	a	t
ASCII Binary Character	1100011	1100001	1110100

The globalization of information has made clear that character sets based only upon English-language characters will not meet the world's needs. Therefore a new standard, Unicode, has been developed with enough capacity to hold all the symbols used in any of the 6,800 languages on the planet. Unicode is already being used in Windows 95, Windows 98, and Windows NT, as well as Office 95 and Office 97.[3]

REPRESENTING IMAGES

Preserving digital information involves more than preserving numbers and text. Archivists and librarians increasingly are dealing with digital images, both those "born digital" and those scanned from originals on paper.

The basic principle in representing images is to divide the page into a fine grid of picture elements, called pixels. To oversimplify, the finer the grid the more image detail that is resolved. In the case of black and white images, each pixel will be captured as either black or white, with nothing in between (remember that digital means discrete states rather than continuously varying waves). With more complex images—those involving shades of gray or color—each pixel will have to represent more than just black or white. The pixel will have a value that translates into "degree of grayness" (for grayscale images) or color (for color images).

- *Grayscale* means that instead of just pure black and white, several shades between white and black are used. For example, 64-level grayscale means that there are 64 different shades of gray between black and white.
- *Color images* involve more than just a single grayscale number for each spot on the grid. Rather, three numbers are required: hue (color), saturation (richness of color), and grayscale (darkness or lightness of the color).[4]

As with text, there are standard ways of representing images. These standards are a key component of a preservation strategy for images, whether still or moving. There are three standard file formats for still images that are most commonly used:

- *Graphics Interchange Format.* GIF was developed by CompuServe. It is especially suited to graphic images like cartoons. It does not support as many colors as some other file formats.
- *Tagged Image File Format.* TIFF was developed by the Aldus Corporation. The major use is for large, high-quality or high-resolution images or photographs. There are some incompatibilities among different versions of TIFF.
- *Joint Photographic Experts Group.* The JPEG File Interchange Format uses a compression scheme that eliminates picture information whose absence our eyes won't detect.

Both TIFF and JPEG, though standards, offer preservation challenges. The incompatibilities among TIFF "flavors" may lessen its suitability as a long-term preservation format.[5] In terms of JPEG, once information is eliminated through compression, it cannot be restored. Compression adds another layer of preservation complexity.[6]

REPRESENTING SOUND

As discussed above, sounds are analog realities that are communicated on waves. When we speak, our vocal cords cause the air to vibrate at a certain frequency. The sound moves through the air on a wave until it reaches the ear of our listener, where the wave is converted into meaning. If we are listening to music on a stereo, the voltage in the speaker wire causes the speaker to vibrate and launch its sound into the air.

These analog sounds must be encoded into digital form to be manipulated by a computer. This is done through a process called *sampling*; the level of the sound on the wave is measured and assigned a numeric value. This numeric value, in turn, is converted to digital form for the computer. On the other end, the digital number is decoded and converted back into an analog form comprehensible to our ears.

Naturally, if only a few samples are taken, the resulting sound will be choppy and far from true-to-life. Sampling for digital conversion involves thousands of sound snapshots each second. In this way, the digital samples, though discrete entities, sound smooth to our ears.

REPRESENTING INSTRUCTIONS

The final items that we must translate into "computerese" are the instructions for the actions we wish the computer to perform. The instructions, called programs, are the heart of computing.

As with all other types of information, the computer's instructions must be stored within the computer's memory before they can be used. Furthermore, they must be stored in binary form. A program is nothing more than a set of binary instructions, which the computer can follow, or execute.

There are various "languages" involved in the process of creating instructions, moving from low-level (the binary code the computer understands) to higher-level (structure and syntax similar to what humans use).[7]

Computer programs have some specific preservation concerns:

- If the data we are trying to preserve will only run using a specific program, we need to preserve either the actual program or the functionality of the program.
- The best way to know how a program is constructed and what it is intended to do is to preserve its "documentation," a code book and other reference materials created by its author.

In conclusion, the computer is a complex machine capable of manipulating various kinds of data. All the data, however, must be stored for both short and long term use. As the next section discusses, this storage employs a number of different media, sizes and formats, all of which present preservation challenges.

PHYSICAL MEDIA

The physical media of the digital world fall into two main categories, magnetic and optical.

- Magnetic media use the principles of electromagnetism to record and change electrical signals.
- Optical media use concentrated light in the form of lasers to alter reflectance on the surface of a disk.

The key is that both media preserve information in two discrete states, corresponding to the ones and zeroes of computer representation. Keeping your ones and your zeroes straight over time is the preservation objective.

MAGNETIC MEDIA

Magnetic recording has dominated computer storage technology since the 1950s.[8] As noted above, magnetic media rely upon temporary magnetism to record and erase the information we wish to store. While the information is active, the computer retrieves information from storage, brings it into the central processing unit, performs the desired operation, and usually returns it to storage.

All magnetic media are composed of three principal layers:

- Recording material
- Substrate
- Binder[9]

The *recording material* must be capable of being magnetized when placed in a magnetic field. The external magnetic field is generated by an electromagnet called a *read/write head*. Just as important, the recording material also needs to retain the magnetism when the field is removed.

This retaining of information is what distinguishes *storage* from *memory*. The latter, often referred to a Random Access Memory (or RAM), is a volatile, temporary holding area that is erased when the computer is turned off.

The *substrate* is the base material upon which the recording material is coated. It is a carrier for the information. Examples of substrate are a nickel-reinforced aluminum platter, a thin ribbon of polyester film, ceramic materials, and glass compounds.

The binder, as the name implies, fastens the recording material to the substrate. It is an essential but often overlooked layer of the magnetic club sandwich.

Chapter 4 discusses what can go wrong with these three layers, each of which will react differently to changes in temperature and humidity. As each individual layer reacts, there also will be tendency toward separation, which certainly will not promote long term preservation.

Magnetic media fall into two categories: disk and tape. Each category has advantages and disadvantages, reasons why you would use it and reasons why you would not. The differences primarily relate to the way one accesses information. The following chart summarizes the differences.

"The vision of creating digital libraries that will be able to preserve our heritage currently rests on technological quicksand. There is as yet no viable long-term strategy to ensure that digital information will be readable in the future. Not only are digital documents vulnerable to loss via media decay and obsolescence, but they become equally inaccessible and unreadable if the software needed to interpret them—or the hardware on which that software runs—is lost or becomes obsolete."—Jeff Rothenberg, *Avoiding Technological Quicksand.*

Category	Type of Access	Explanation of Access	Analogies	Applications
Disk	Random	The user can access any location quickly, at random	A track on a phonograph record; a restaurant menu from which you can select any item	Active files and programs
Tape	Serial	The user must access information in sequence, going past previous locations on the tape	A song on a cassette tape; a buffet line that moves past various food choices before you can select lunch	Backups and off-line inactive storage

Magnetic Hard Drives

Magnetic hard drives are essential components of today's personal computers. To quote Ron White:

A hard drive is the workaholic of a PC system. The platters on which data is stored spin at speeds of up to 7,200 revolutions a minute—120 spins each second. Each time the hard drive is accessed to read or save a file it causes the read/write heads to burst into a furious flurry of movement that must be performed with microscopic precision. So exacting are the tolerances in a hard drive—the gaps between the heads and the platters aren't big enough to admit a human hair—that it's a wonder the drive can perform its work at all without constant disasters. Instead, it keeps on plugging away as the repository of perhaps years of work—with surprisingly few failures.[10]

Hard disks are made from polished aluminum platters. After polishing, the disks are coated one at a time with a thin layer of magnetic material, then they are used either singly or in stacks.

The principal advantage of magnetic hard drives is that they offer rapid, direct access to information, especially when compared to magnetic tape. Hard drives are formatted into a series of tracks and sectors into which information is placed:

- *Tracks* are concentric circles around the disk.
- *Sectors* are located on the tracks and hold the information. Sectors have gaps between them.

Disk systems do not store records together physically. Parts of a record may be scattered all over the disk. To locate these scattered parts, the disk includes a listing of addresses on the outermost track. A controller consults this subdirectory and reassembles the file in the correct order before sending it on to the central processing unit (CPU).

When a file is deleted from a disk, the sectors involved are labeled as "empty" in the directory. However, the old data remain unchanged until new data are stored in their place. Thus, accidentally "erased" files can still be retrieved by using a program that bypasses the directory to find the desired data sector by sector.

Most hard drives still use the so-called Winchester Technology introduced by IBM in the 1970s. Winchester drives took their name from an internal IBM product designation.

A Winchester drive contains one or more magnetic disk platters and read/write mechanisms in a sealed module. This structure enhances reliability, minimizes contamination, and virtually eliminates preventive maintenance. If you look inside a personal computer, you will not see a magnetic hard drive *per se*. What you will see is a Winchester-type assembly connected by cables to the motherboard of the computer.

There are two other important terms relating to magnetic disks: DASD and RAID:

- *DASD* stands for Direct Access Storage Devices. DASD employs large platters (mostly 14-inch platters) and is used in large computer installations. It is being replaced by multidrive arrays with small disks.
- *RAID* stands for Redundant Array of Inexpensive Disks. This technology combines multiple hard drives to create reliable, high-capacity computer storage configurations. The computer stores data on more than one disk, enabling one to avoid or minimize downtime and the risk of data loss if one of the disks fails.[11]

Removable Hard Drives. In 1988 manufacturers introduced removable hard drive systems. It now became possible to remove hard drives to increase security (by locking drives) or expand capacity (by exchanging them). Removable hard drives usually are supplements to fixed hard drives rather than replacements for them.

Floppy Disks. Floppy disks are the most widely encountered type of removable magnetic media. They were introduced in 1971 and became an instant success with consumers. Floppy disks have a lower recording density than hard disks. However, they are rugged and can be easily removed from one computer's disk drive and placed in that of another computer. We already have seen technology change as 8-inch floppy disks have given way first to $5^{1}/_{4}$-inch disks and now to $3^{1}/_{2}$-inch disks.

The changes in floppy disk sizes and formats are a precursor of larger preservation challenges to come. Many of us have experienced first-hand the need to access files on an old floppy disk that is unreadable on our new computer equipment. This is the same issue our organizations are likely to face, on a broader scale, as entire information systems are replaced with increasing frequency.

Magnetic Tapes

Magnetic tape is the most widely used medium for offline data storage and backup protection. It is a long strip of polyester film coated with a magnetizable recording material. As noted above, magnetic tape uses sequential access to information.

A disadvantage of magnetic tape is the time required to find data after it has been stored. Searching a long tape for a particular file, even though it is all stored together, typically takes much longer than finding the same file scattered about the surface of a disk. Thousands of feet of tape may have to pass the read/write head before the desired information comes along.[12]

There are two methods of recording information on magnetic tape:

- *Longitudinal recording* stores information in tracks that run along the length of the tape.
- *Helical scan recording* uses technologies adapted from video and audio recording. Two or more magnetic heads record data in narrow tracks positioned at an acute angle with respect to the edges of the tape.

Longitudinal Recording Formats. The most common longitudinal recording formats are reel-to-reel 9-track tape, 3480/3490 cartridge, QIC (quarter-inch cartridge), and DLT (digital linear tape).

Reel-to-Reel 9-Track Tape. Nine-track reel-to-reel tapes are composed of half-inch tape wound on plastic reels. The most widely used reels measure 10.5 inches in diameter and contain 2,400 feet of tape. Across the width of the tape, bits that encode individual characters are recorded in nine parallel tracks: eight tracks store data bits that encode characters, while the ninth track is reserved for a parity bit that reduces recording and playback errors.

Nine-track reels are far from a cutting edge technology and certainly do not have the data storage capacity of newer magnetic media. Why, then, are they still in use? The reason is that nine-track reels are a mature technology with little likelihood of discontinuation. They offer excellent compatibility of equipment and recording media. Using nine-track reels minimizes future problems of backward compatibility associated with computer storage technologies that are subject to continuing development. This makes them a popular choice for data archiving.[13]

3480/3490 Cartridge. The 3480/3490 cartridges are a compact, convenient, higher capacity alternative to nine-track reels. They use half-inch magnetic tape packaged in a plastic cartridge measuring 4" x 5" x 1". The tape features a chromium-dioxide recording layer.

This format became popular after IBM introduced its 3480 Magnetic Tape Cartridge Subsystem in 1984. The 3480 cartridge is divided into two parallel sets of nine tracks each, for a total of 18 tracks recorded in a longitudinal format. One set of tracks is recorded from beginning to end using $1/4$ inch of tape. The tape then is rewound and the other set of tracks is recorded from beginning to end. This process is also called serpentine recording.[14]

In 1995, IBM introduced the 3590 cartridge. The 3590 is identical in size to the 3480, but has a higher recording density. Taken together, the cartridges are called the 34xx formats. There are various national and international standards for unrecorded cartridges and a large installed base. An advantage of the 3590 is that automated tape libraries are available for faster handling of cartridges. Another plus is that drive manufacturers routinely provide backward compatibility as they introduce newer products.

Since the 1980s, half-inch cartridges have supplanted nine-track reels as the magnetic tape format of choice for data archiving. Half-inch cartridges require less shelf space than nine-track reels to store the same amount of data. Stated differently, conversion to half-inch cartridges can expand a vault's capacity. In addition, as will be discussed in Chapter 4, half-inch cartridges require less maintenance time from the preservation administrator.

Quarter-Inch Cartridge (QIC). Quarter-inch cartridges, which were introduced in the early 1970s, are the most complicated and diverse group of magnetic tape products. Quarter-inch "cartridges" actually are cassettes: both a supply spool and a take-up spool are inside the plastic case.

QIC formats all employ serpentine, longitudinal recording on parallel tracks. They come in two sizes:

- $5^1/4$-inch cartridges are called Data Cartridges (DC)
- $3^1/2$-inch cartridges are called Mini-Cartridges (MC)

High-capacity QIC minicartridge standards are called MC3000-class formats and are based on 3M media designations.

Digital Linear Tape (DLT). Digital Linear Tape is another half-inch data cartridge technology. It was introduced in the early 1990s by Digital Equipment Corporation (DEC) as a higher capacity alternative to the 34xx formats. The cartridges are the same size as 34xx cartridges.

Helical Scan Recording Formats. As noted above, helical scan recording uses technologies adapted from video and audio recording. Two or more magnetic heads record data in narrow tracks positioned at an acute angle to the edges of the tape. Helical scan recordings offer higher densities than longitudinal recordings. The most widely encountered helical scan recording formats are eight-millimeter data cartridges and digital audiotape (DAT).[15]

Eight-Millimeter Data Cartridges. In 1987 Exabyte introduced data cartridges based upon eight-millimeter video cassette technology. The cartridges, which are actually cassettes, measure 3.7" x 2.5" x 0.6". The cartridges contain a metal-particle tape specifically designed for high-density data recording. These sometimes are called D8 Tapes.

Digital Audio Tape (DAT). Digital Audio Tape was introduced in 1988. It is based on technology originally developed for audio rather than video recording. The recording tape is four millimeters wide and is housed in a cassette measuring 3" x 2" x 0.4".

OPTICAL MEDIA

Optical media employ a different technology from that used for magnetic disks and tapes. Optical media use light generated by lasers to record and retrieve information. They record information by altering the light-reflectance characteristics of a given medium: reflecting light a certain way equals a "one," while reflecting light a different way equals a "zero."

One category of optical disk is called WORM: Write-Once, Read Many. Recording information on these disks requires the following:

- Disk material with reflectance that can be permanently altered by a laser beam
- A laser operating at two power levels: high for recording, low for reading

Other technologies are used for rewritable optical disks.

Altering Reflectance

Optical disk systems alter reflectance in one of six ways:

- Ablative recording
- Thermal-bubble recording
- Dual-alloy recording
- Dye-based recording
- Magneto-optical recording
- Phase change recording[16]

Figure 2.2   Optical Disk Recording

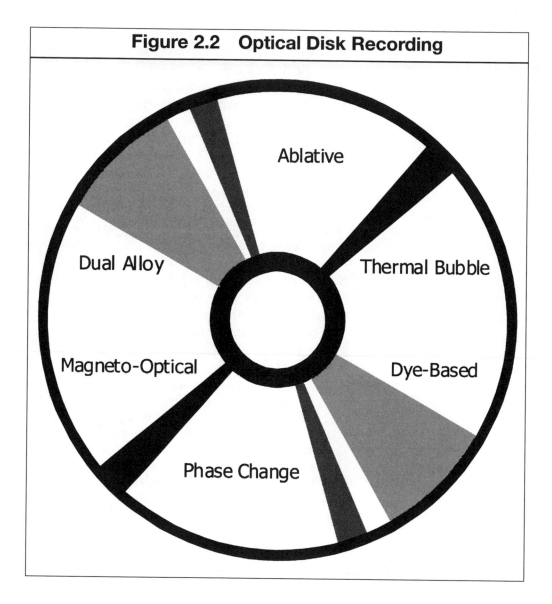

Ablative Recording. With ablative recording, the laser changes reflectance by burning a pit into the disk. This process is called *ablation*. To record information on a tellurium-seleniun alloy disk, a laser shines through the protective layers of glass to melt holes in the underlying alloy. When read, the holes are less reflective than their surroundings.

Thermal-Bubble Recording. In the thermal-bubble approach, heat from a laser evaporates a polymer layer to form bubbles in a thin film composed of precious metals, such as gold or platinum. These bubbles open up to reveal an underlayer with different reflectance properties.

Dual-Alloy Recording. In another type of WORM disk, heat from a laser shining through a plastic base fuses two layers of antimony-selenium alloy with one of bismuth-tellurium alloy. A metallic plug forms, which, during reading, is more transparent to laser light than is the surrounding unfused area.

Dye-Based Recording. Dye-based recording features a transparent polymer layer that contains an infrared-absorbing dye. This recording layer is coated on a plastic or glass substrate. The laser induces a diffusion of the dye into an absorption layer, producing detectable differences in the reflectance of diffused and pure dye areas.

Magneto-Optical Recording. As the name implies, magneto-optical recording uses both magnetic and optical properties to record and erase data. Magneto-optical media store information magnetically, but the information is recorded and read by a laser and optical assembly.

Magneto-optical alloys have inherent magnetism, like ordinary bar magnets. At room temperature, they are highly resistant to any change in the magnetic field. But at a spot where a recording laser heats them, the inherent direction of the magnetization can be reversed by an external magnetic field.

To accomplish this, a highly focused laser beam heats a spot on a disk to its Curie temperature, the point at which the medium's magnetic orientation is lost. The change in magnetism of the recorded spot causes it to shift the polarization of a reflected beam slightly, enabling the disk to be read by a special detector system. The spots can be erased by reheating them in the presence of a reversed magnetic field.

Phase-Change Recording. The last technology depends on alterations in crystal structure. With phase-change recording, a laser switches certain metals between a highly reflective crystalline phase and a less reflective noncrystalline (amorphous) phase. As with all of the above, the difference in reflectance is used to distinguish between ones and zeroes. Phase change recording can be either write-once or rewritable technology.

William Saffady has pointed out the preservation problems inherent in WORM technologies that vendors no longer support:

> Of these five WORM technologies [ablative recording, dye-based recording, phase-change recording, thermal-bubble recording, and dual-alloy recording], only dye-based recording, which is used by compact disk-recordable (CD-R) systems, was widely implemented at the time of this writing. Since the mid-1990s, several dozen WORM products have been discontinued, as users accustomed to magnetic media increasingly prefer rewritable optical disks. Because

"Many archivists and records managers have an immediate response to the words *imaging* or *optical disc*: they cringe. Too many stories—and sometimes personal experiences—focusing on failed systems, inaccessible records, and long-term storage problems have soured many records professionals on the promise of imaging."—Michael L. Miller, "Disc Players, the Records Manager/Archivist, and the Development of Optical Imaging Applications."

many WORM products are proprietary, information recorded on discontinued media is unreadable.[17]

Compact Disc

The phrase "compact disc" means that the system uses optical storage formats and products based on technology developed jointly by Sony and Philips during the 1970s and 1980s. Compact discs have a reflective metal layer covered with a protective coating. Information is recorded as microscopic pits and adjoining spaces arranged in spiraling tracks.

CD-ROM stands for Compact Disc-Read Only Memory. CD-ROM is the application of compact disc technology to the storage of computer-processible information. CD-ROMs measure 4.75 inches in diameter. The principal advantages of CD-ROMs are their relatively low cost, widespread availability, and established international standards.

Another option, Compact Disc-Recordable (CD-R), became available in the late 1980s. CD-Rs permit direct recording of information on Compact Disc without going through the mastering process that previously was necessary. CD-Rs can store over 600 megabytes of data but offer slower access times than other types of optical disks.

Optical Media

Optical media use substrates of metal, glass, or plastic. The disks usually are enclosed in plastic cartridges for protection. The information-bearing surface is divided into tracks, like a magnetic disk. The disks often are combined into juke boxes. Optical disks are available in write-once and rewritable formats.

There have been various sizes for optical disks:

- 14 inch
- 12 inch
- $5^{1}/_{4}$ inch
- $3^{1}/_{2}$ inch

The general trend in size has been similar to that with magnetic media: larger disks are being replaced by smaller ones. In the mid-1980s, 14-inch disks were introduced for high-volume data storage. The commercial success of the 1980s, however, was the 12-inch optical disk, especially when combined in a juke box. Beginning in 1983, $5^{1}/_{4}$-inch optical disks became available and now can be purchased in write-once, rewritable, and multifunction configurations.

CONCLUSION

Digital information is complex. Not only must we take our familiar world and convert it into the ones and zeroes of the digital domain, but we then must store the resulting representation on something quite different from our familiar paper.

Archivists and preservation administrators have been trying to deal with this complexity in a number of ways. First and foremost, they have conducted research to develop a framework for understanding and action. The next chapter summarizes the best of this research.

NOTES

1. For a very good discussion of representation, see Kurt F. Laukner and Mildred D. Lintner, *The Computer Continuum* (Indianapolis: Que Education and Training, Macmillan, 1999), Chapter 2. Much of the section which follows is based upon Laukner and Lintner.

2. A true base 12 would require 12 distinct symbols. Since we only have 10 symbols in our numbering system (0–9), we would have to add two more with agreed-upon values. Computers do use a system called hexadecimal numbers to keep from having to process long strings of ones and zeros. Hexadecimal numbers use base 16. Since we only have ten numerals (0–9), the hexadecimal system adds six other characters (A, B, C, D, E, F). The resulting "number" looks very strange to us, since it combines numerals and characters.

3. For more on Unicode, see Peter Norton and John Goodman, *Peter Norton's Inside the PC,* 8th Ed. (Indianapolis: Sams Publishing, Macmillan, 1999), 55–58.

4. The Internet contains many sources of information about scanning of images. For a beginning point, see "Scanning 101" at *w102.web2010.com/scantips/www.index.html* and "Scanning Basics" at *home.cc.umanitoba.ca/~hounslow/scanning.basics.html.*

5. The State of Ohio stated the problem as follows: "Many digital imaging systems use the Tagged Image File Format or TIFF. Because different versions of TIFF exist, there is still no absolute guarantee that images can be transported seamlessly from one system to another. Comprehensive documentation of the digital image file format, including TIFF, is recommended." State of Ohio, "Digital Document Imaging: Guidelines for State of Ohio Execu-

tive Agencies," November 1999, available online at: *www.ohiojunction.net/erc/imaging/imagingguidelines.html*. Page updated 2/22/00.

6. For more on image formats, see Laukner and Lintner, Chapter 10. See also Lisa L. Macklin and Sarah L. Lockmiller, *Digital Imaging of Photographs: A Practical Approach to Workflow Design and Project Management* (Chicago: American Library Association, 1999), 23–24.

7. For a detailed discussion of computer languages, see Laukner and Lintner, Chapter 5.

8. For a thorough treatment of storage media and other issues, see William Saffady, *Managing Electronic Records*, 2nd ed. (Prairie Village, KS: ARMA International, 1998). Saffady is particularly good on the historical development of formats and the evolution of storage capacities. Much of the following review is based upon pages 19–51. For another discussion of technology with more of an international perspective, see Advisory Committee for the Coordination of Information Systems (ACCIS), *Optical Storage: An Overview of the Technology and Its Use within the United Nations System* (New York: United Nations, 1993).

9. For an excellent treatment of magnetic media, especially from a preservation perspective, see John W. C. Van Bogart, *Magnetic Tape Storage and Handling: A Guide for Libraries and Archives* (Washington, DC: Commission on Preservation and Access; St. Paul, MN: National Media Laboratory, 1995).

10. Ron White, *How Computers Work* (Emeryville, CA: Ziff-Davis, 1997), 83.

11. For more on RAID, see Norton, 261; White, 86–87. RAID can also stand for Redundant Array of Independent Disks.

12. See *Understanding Computers: Memory and Storage* (Alexandria, VA: Time-Life, 1990), 64–66.

13. Saffady, *Managing Electronic Records*, 29.

14. Saffady, *Managing Electronic Records*, 30.

15. Saffady, *Managing Electronic Records*, 34.

16. Much of the following section is based upon *Understanding Computers*, 118–121. See also William Saffady, *Electronic Document Imaging Systems: Design, Evaluation, and Implementation* (Westport, CT: Meckler, 1993), 64–72.

17. Saffady, *Managing Electronic Records*, 44.

3 RECENT RESEARCH IN ELECTRONIC RECORDS AND DIGITAL PRESERVATION

The last ten years have been fertile ground for research into electronic records and digital preservation. As a result, the archivist, records manager, or preservation administrator facing the digital challenge has a firm research foundation upon which to build his or her efforts. The frameworks and approaches developed and tested during these research projects have become invaluable tools in the preservation toolbox.

This chapter will review some of the recent initiatives; many more are included in the bibliography. The eight discussed here are:

- University of British Columbia
- U.S. Department of Defense
- Uniform Electronic Transactions Act
- University of Pittsburgh
- Universal Preservation Format
- Rand Corporation
- Digital Library Federation
- InterPARES

UNIVERSITY OF BRITISH COLUMBIA

From 1994 to 1997, the University of British Columbia's (UBC) School of Library, Archival, and Information Studies conducted a research project titled "The Preservation of the Integrity of Electronic Records." The purpose of the project was to identify and define the requirements for creating, handling, and preserving reliable and authentic electronic records. The research team consisted of Luciana Duranti, principal investigator; Terry Eastwood, co-investigator; and Heather MacNeil, research assistant. The project was funded by the Social Sciences and Humanities Research Council of Canada.[1]

The specific objectives of the research project were to

- establish what a record is in principle and how it can be recognized in an electronic environment;
- determine what kinds of electronic systems generate records;
- formulate criteria that allow for the segregation of records from all other types of information in electronic systems;
- define the conceptual requirements for guaranteeing the reliability and authenticity of records in electronic systems;
- assess these requirements against different administrative, juridical, cultural, and disciplinary points of view.

The UBC team took a deductive approach to the project—they began with a set of general premises and considered whether these premises held up in particular instances. The theoretical basis for the general premises was provided by the principles of diplomatics[2] and archival science.[3]

Central to the UBC research was the distinction between reliability and authenticity:

- *Reliability* refers to a record's authority and trustworthiness. This concept is tied to records creation and means that the record is able "to stand for the fact it is about." The content in a reliable record is trustworthy.[4]
- *Authenticity* refers to a record's reliability over time. It is linked to the record's status, mode, and form of transmission and the manner of its preservation and custody. Authentic records are genuine.[5]

The findings of the research project fell into two categories. The first category involved specific methods for ensuring the reliability and authenticity of electronic records. This is best assured by

- embedding procedural rules in the overall records system and by integrating business and documentary procedures;
- emphasizing the documentary context of the electronic records;
- managing the electronic records together with all related records.

The second category of findings involved management issues that are part of the maintenance and preservation of reliable and authentic records. They found the following two principles:

- There are two managerial phases, one involving active and semiactive records, and the other involving inactive records.
- Entrusting the creating body with responsibility for reliability and the preserving body with responsibility for authenticity best preserves the integrity of electronic records.

"Deciding which records warrant preservation will become more critical because a much smaller percentage of documentary evidence will survive despite declining storage costs."—Margaret Hedstrom, "Electronic Archives: Integrity and Access in the Network Environment," *American Archivist* 58 (Summer 1995), 312.

"Preservation of the media and of the software technologies will serve only part of the need if the information content has been corrupted from its original form, whether by accident or design. The need for intellectual preservation arises because the great asset of digital information is also its great liability: the ease with which an identical copy can be quickly and flawlessly made is paralleled by the ease with which a change may undetectably be made." Peter S. Graham, *Intellectual Preservation: Electronic Preservation of the Third Kind.*

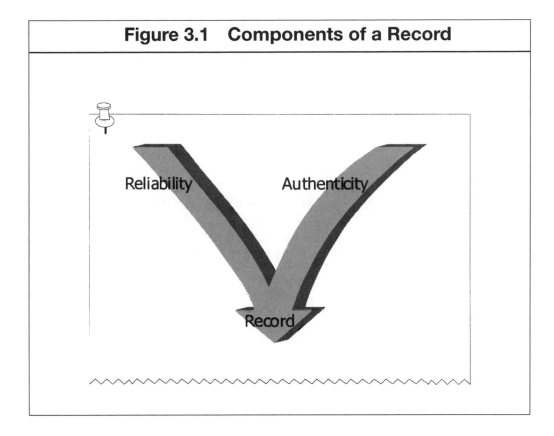

Figure 3.1   Components of a Record

The UBC team also collaborated with the U.S. Department of Defense (DoD) Records Management Task Force. The task force sought to develop requirements for records management support systems, both electronic and nonelectronic. The UBC and DoD teams used standard modeling techniques to relate archival and diplomatic concepts to DoD needs. The collaboration developed a series of rules that became the basis for the "Design Criteria Standard for Electronic Records Management Software Applications" discussed in the next section.

U.S. DEPARTMENT OF DEFENSE

Because of its vast size, the United States Department of Defense (DoD) needed to make certain that electronic documents remained readable for their full retention period. In addition to preservation, DoD also wanted to make certain that electronic documents were managed as efficiently as possible.

In November 1997, the assistant secretary of defense for Command, Control, Communications, and Intelligence issued a document called "Design Criteria Standard for Electronic Records Management Software Applications." This standard was given the number "DoD 5015.2-STD."[6]

This standard established the baseline functional requirements for Records Management Application (RMA) software. DoD defines a records management application as "software used by an organization to manage its records." Its primary management functions are categorizing and locating records and identifying records that are due for disposition. RMA software also stores, retrieves, and disposes of the electronic records that are stored in its repository.

The following are among the main functional requirements that the DoD established for Records Management Applications:

- RMAs shall assign a unique identifier to each record they manage.
- RMAs shall prevent subsequent changes to documents that have been designated as records. The content of the record, once filed, shall be preserved.
- RMAs must be able to assign a minimum metadata profile when the record is filed.
- RMAs shall link supporting and related records and related information such as notes, marginalia, attachments, and electronic mail return receipts, as well as all profile data, to the record.
- RMAs shall not alter nor allow alteration of records they store. They shall preserve the format and content of the record as it was filed.
- RMAs shall provide the capability to track automatically the disposition schedules of records.
- RMAs shall delete records or profiles that are stored in their repositories and that have been approved for destruction in a manner such that the records cannot be physically reconstructed.

Since RMAs are prohibited from altering the format of stored records, the organization must ensure that it has the ability to view, copy, print and, if appropriate, process any record stored in RMAs for as long as that record must be retained. The DoD standard gives the organization four options for meeting this requirement:

1. Maintain the hardware and/or software used to create or capture the record.
2. Maintain hardware and/or software capable of viewing the record in its native format.

"Often, some people assume that with enough finagling, it is possible to work around the incompatibility problems between older and newer formats, but this is not always the case. Complex documents, particularly those that include graphics and tables may convert very poorly, some not at all, and some may actually become corrupted."—Rich Lysakowski and Zahava Leibowitz, *Titanic 2020: A Call to Action.*

3. Ensure downward compatibility when hardware and/or software is updated.
4. Migrate the record to a new format before the old format becomes obsolete.

The DoD standard has important implications for organizations of all size, both inside and outside of the federal government:

- Once DoD establishes a standard, vendors are likely to offer products that meet the requirements because of DoD's large purchasing power.
- DoD already has established a testing program to certify vendor products that meet the standard. A list of compliant vendors is available on the Internet.
- Other organizations can make the DoD standard part of their own requirements in requests for proposals that they issue to vendors.

DoD 5015.2 is an important milestone in the effort to preserve digital information. For the first time, standards have been established by an organization with enough purchasing clout to force vendor compliance. All other organizations trying to preserve digital information can benefit from this DoD initiative.

UNIFORM ELECTRONIC TRANSACTIONS ACT

Another way to establish common practice is through a "uniform law." These uniform or model laws are drafted by experts and then offered to the states for adoption. If enough states adopt the uniform law, then legal practice becomes more consistent across the country.

In July 1999, the National Conference of Commissioners on Uniform State Laws approved the Uniform Electronic Transactions Act (UETA).[7] The act is intended to apply to "any electronic record or electronic signature created, generated, sent, communicated, received, or stored."

One of the main purposes of the UETA is to provide legal recognition of four situations common in the digital world.

1. A record or signature may not be denied legal effect or enforceability solely because it is in electronic form.

"Clearly a book and a digital document are different kinds of knowledge artifacts, and those differences will have consequences for the way ideas are written and read, but they are not opposites."—Peter Lyman, "What Is a Digital Library?

2. A contract may not be denied legal effect or enforceability solely because an electronic record was used in its formation.
3. If a law requires a record to be in writing, an electronic record satisfies the law.
4. If a law requires a signature, an electronic signature satisfies the law.

It is important to note that the UETA does not *require* records to be created or received in electronic form. Rather, it *permits* electronic records and electronic transactions to be used by parties that wish to do so.

The UETA has a section that deals specifically with the retention of electronic records. According to Section 12, if a law requires that a record be retained, the requirement is satisfied by retaining an electronic record which:

1. "accurately reflects the information set forth in the record after it was first generated in its final form as an electronic record or otherwise."
2. "remains accessible for later reference."

The section further states that if a law requires a record to be retained in its original form, the law is satisfied by the retention of an electronic record that meets the above two conditions. Finally for our purposes, Section 13 covers admissibility in evidence, stating that a record may not be excluded solely because it is in electronic form.[8]

As the UETA is adopted across the country, we can expect increasing interest in the preservation of information in electronic form. Once the main legal issues are resolved, organizations of all sizes will rely more and more on their electronic records. There is every reason to expect that preservation of digital information will grow in importance.

UNIVERSITY OF PITTSBURGH

In 1993 the University of Pittsburgh's School of Information Studies received a three-year grant from the National Historical Publications and Records Administration (NHPRC), a Division of the National Archives and Records Administration. This project researched variables that affect the integration of recordkeeping requirements for evidence into electronic systems. The project generated four main outcomes:

- Recordkeeping functional requirements (defining records);
- Production rules to support the requirements (making the functional requirements unambiguous and implementable);
- Metadata specifications for recordkeeping (providing a software-independent way to encapsulate records);
- Literary warrant (reflecting the professional and societal endorsement of the concept of recordkeeping functional requirements).[9]

The first project result, the recordkeeping functional requirements, addressed some of the same issues as those researched at the University of British Columbia. As Richard Cox stated, "In one sense both projects were part of a refocusing on the fundamentals of what constitutes a record and how such a definition of *record* could better facilitate the management of electronic information systems increasingly being used to create and keep records."

The following is an abbreviated version of the "Functional Requirements for Evidence in Recordkeeping." This is a statement of the requirements for ensuring the preservation of evidence in electronic form. Although specifically related to electronic recordkeeping systems, the requirements are also applicable to manual or hybrid systems.[10]

ORGANIZATION: CONSCIENTIOUS

1. *Compliant.* Organizations must comply with the legal and administrative requirements for recordkeeping within the jurisdictions in which they operate, and they must demonstrate awareness of best practices for the industry or business sector to which they belong and the business functions in which they are engaged.

RECORDKEEPING SYSTEMS: ACCOUNTABLE

2. *Responsible.* Recordkeeping systems must have accurately documented policies, assigned responsibilities, and formal methodologies for their management.
3. *Implemented.* Recordkeeping systems must be employed at all times in the normal course of business.
4. *Consistent.* Recordkeeping systems must process information in a fashion that assures that the records they create are credible.

RECORDS: CAPTURED

5. *Comprehensive.* Records must be created for all business transactions.
6. *Identifiable.* Records must be bounded by linkage to a transaction that used all the data in the record and only that data.
7. *Complete.* Records must contain the content, structure, and context generated by the transaction they document.
8. *Authorized.* An authorized record creator must have originated all records.

RECORDS: MAINTAINED

9. *Preserved.* Records must continue to reflect content, structure, and context within any systems by which the records are retained over time.
10. *Removable.* Record content and the structure supporting the meaning of content must be deletable.

RECORDS: USABLE

11. *Exportable.* It must be possible to transmit records to other systems without loss of information.
12. *Accessible.* It must be possible to output record content, structure, and context.
13. *Redactable.* Records must be masked when it is necessary to deliver censored copies, and the version as released must be documented in a linked transaction.

These functional requirements were a significant step in the development of thinking about preserving digital information. There have been a number of projects to test the functional requirements in different organizational settings.[11] What these tests have shown is that the functional requirements are not an "all or nothing" proposition. Rather, they are guidelines that an organization can use and adapt as necessary to meet its needs. This is the key point for any organization looking to preserve digital information. The University of Pittsburgh Functional Requirements remain a succinct statement of what a digital preservation program is designed to achieve.

> "The essence of preserving informational artifacts is the retention of their meaning. This requires the ability to recreate the original form and function of a document when it is accessed, for example, to establish its authenticity, validity, and evidential value and to allow the document's users to understand how its creator and original viewers saw it, what they were (and were not) able to infer from it, what insights it may have conveyed to them, and what aesthetic value it may have had for them."—Jeff Rothenberg, *Avoiding Technological Quicksand: Finding a Viable Technical Foundation for Digital Preservation.*

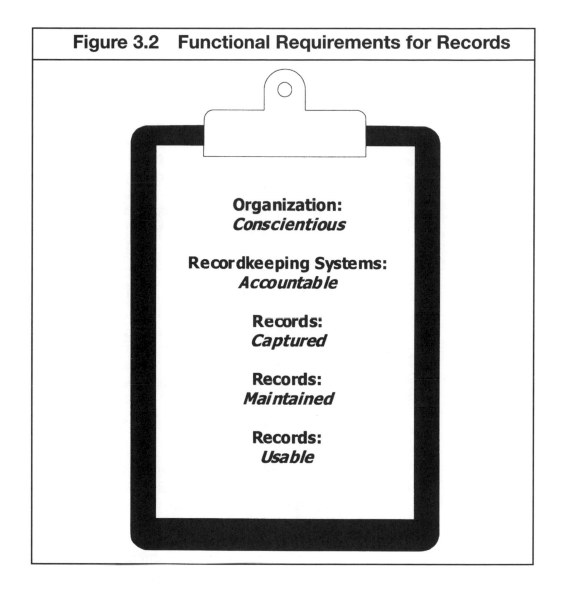

Figure 3.2   Functional Requirements for Records

Organization:
Conscientious

Recordkeeping Systems:
Accountable

Records:
Captured

Records:
Maintained

Records:
Usable

UNIVERSAL PRESERVATION FORMAT

In 1997, the WGBH Educational Foundation received a grant from the National Historical Publications and Records Commission (NHRPC) to investigate a "Universal Preservation Format" (UPF). The UPF is a data file mechanism that utilizes a container or wrapper structure. The UPF is designed to be independent of

- the computer applications that created them;
- the operating system from which the applications originated;
- the physical media upon which they are stored.

The UPF is characterized as "self-described" because it includes within its metadata all the technical specifications required to rebuild appropriate media browsers to access its contents into the future.

But the UPF is more than just a technical project. In the words of the project team, "the UPF initiative helps establish working relationships between those who make and market technical specifications and those who must learn to use the tools of technology to preserve the rapidly decaying fruits of our cultural heritage."[12] This is perhaps the initiative's greatest contribution to date. It has opened a wide-ranging discussion among content providers, administrators, computer professionals, archivists, and preservation administrators.

RAND CORPORATION

Jeff Rothenberg, a senior research scientist at the Rand Corporation, recently completed a study for the Council on Library and Information Resources. The study, *Avoiding Technological Quicksand: Finding a Viable Technical Foundation for Digital Preservation*, proposes a strategy of emulating obsolete systems on future, unknown systems.[13]

Rothenberg is pessimistic about current preservation strategies. In his words:

> The vision of creating digital libraries that will be able to preserve our heritage currently rests on technological quicksand. There is as yet no viable long-term strategy to ensure that digital information will be readable in the future. Not only are digital documents vulnerable to loss via media decay and obsolescence, but they become equally inaccessible and unreadable if the software needed to interpret them—or the hardware on which that software runs—is lost or becomes obsolete.[14]

Rothenberg believes that current approaches to digital preservation have major shortcomings:

- *Printing and saving documents in hard-copy form.* Rothenberg calls this a "rear-guard action and not a true solution." Printing any but the simplest documents leads to the loss of unique digital functionality and attributes. It also renders the documents unreadable by computer and may affect their historical significance.
- *Relying on standards to keep documents readable.* Standards sow the seeds of their own destruction by encouraging vendors

to implement features that go beyond the standards in order to secure market share. In addition, as new standards develop, they do not always subsume the earlier standard. Finally, it is common to have errors in any translation.

- *Reading documents by running obsolete hardware and software preserved in museums.* It is unlikely that old machines could be kept running indefinitely at any reasonable cost. Even if they could be kept running, access to the original forms of digital documents would be limited to only a few sites in the world.

- *Translating documents so they "migrate" into forms accessible by future generations of software.* According to Rothenberg, "In the long run, migration promises to be expensive, unscalable, error-prone, at most partially successful, and ultimately infeasible."

To summarize Rothenberg's argument, all of the above are "labor-intensive and ultimately incapable of preserving digital documents in their original form."

Rothenberg then outlines the criteria for an ideal solution:

An ideal approach should provide a single, extensible, long-term solution that can be designed once and for all and applied uniformly, automatically, and in synchrony (for example, at every future refresh cycle) to all types of documents and all media, with minimal human intervention. It should provide maximum leverage, in the sense that implementing it for any document type should make it usable for all document types. It should facilitate document management (cataloging, deaccessioning, and so forth) by associating human-readable labeling information and metadata with each document. It should retain as much as desired (and feasible) of the original functionality, look, and feel of each original document, while minimizing translation so as to minimize both labor and the potential for loss via corruption. If translation is unavoidable (as when translating labeling information), the approach should guarantee that this translation will be reversible, so that the original form can be recovered without loss.[15]

In Rothenberg's view, the best long-term solution is to run the original software "under emulation" on future computers. Emulation means that one computer system will act like another. We already experience this when our personal computer emulates, or acts like, a "dumb terminal" into a mainframe system. According to Rothenberg, emulation is the "only reliable way to recreate a digital document's original functionality, look, and feel."

"The combined problems of immense volume, unstable storage media, and obsolete software and hardware add up to some very tough problems for the archivist to deal with. If we take our archival functions seriously, we will have to bring a high-level of sophistication to research in order to develop strategies for dealing effectively with digital media."—William J. Mitchell, "Architectural Archives in the Digital Era."

The implementation of this approach involves developing techniques for:

- specifying emulators that will run on unknown future computers;
- saving in human-readable form the metadata needed to find, access, and recreate digital documents so that emulation techniques can be used for preservation;
- encapsulating documents with their attendant metadata, software, and emulator specifications.

Rothenberg acknowledges that emulation solutions require additional research and proof of feasibility before they can be implemented. Nevertheless, he believes we must devote the time to this approach:

The long-term digital preservation problem calls for a long-lived solution that does not require continual heroic effort or repeated invention of new approaches every time formats, software or hardware paradigms, document types, or recordkeeping practices change. This approach must be extensible, since we cannot predict future changes, and it must not require labor-intensive translation or examination of individual documents. It must handle current and future documents of unknown type in a uniform way, while being capable of evolving as necessary. Furthermore, it should allow flexible choices and tradeoffs among priorities such as access, fidelity, and ease of document management.[16]

An emulation strategy, as proposed by Rothenberg, may be the ultimate long-term solution to the digital preservation problem. In the short term, however, most organizations will be forced to implement some of the solutions that Rothenberg sees as inadequate. Perhaps Rothenberg's most immediate impact upon these organizations will be to remind them about how fleeting even today's best preservation efforts may be.

DIGITAL LIBRARY FEDERATION

The Digital Library Federation (DLF) was founded in 1995 to establish the conditions for creating, maintaining, expanding, and preserving a distributed collection of digital materials accessible to scholars, students, and the wider public. The federation is a leadership organization operating under the umbrella of the Council on Library and

Information Resources. It is composed of participants who manage and operate digital libraries.[17]

The DLF originally had 16 participating institutions, a number that has expanded since 1995. DLF participants have been acting quickly to build the infrastructure and the institutional capacity to sustain digital libraries. Only in 1999 did the DLF add a publication program to disseminate information more broadly. There have been two publications to date: *Enabling Access: A Report on a Workshop on Access Management* and *Preserving the Whole: A Two-Track Approach to Rescuing Social Sciences Data and Metadata.*[18]

More important than its own publications have been the DLF's major collaborative initiatives. Among these have been:[19]

- *Academic Image Cooperative.* An exploration of the ways of using digital libraries to enhance the quality of art history courses in the nation's colleges and universities.
- *Asset Management.* A test of digital certificates and other approaches to licensing digital materials.
- *Digital Archiving.* A review of emulation, migration, and conversion services.
- *Discovery and Retrieval (Metadata).* The development of descriptive standards, distributed finding aids, and common editorial practice.
- *Digital Imaging.* A review of imaging technologies and the development of recommendations for the community.
- *Digital Library Architecture.* A survey of recent literature on the systems architecture of digital libraries.

As noted in Chapter 1, there is a great deal of overlap among those working on digital archives and digital libraries. The DLF initiatives noted above will be reporting significant results over the next few years. Archivists as well as librarians should make the homepage of DLF a regular stop on their Internet tours.

INTERPARES

The most ambitious research initiative is also one of the most recent. It is called the InterPARES Project (International Research on Permanent Authentic Records in Electronic Systems). *Inter pares* is also Latin for "amongst peers," an appropriate name given the collaborative nature of the project.[20]

The project grew out of the research conducted at the University of

"Because of the rapid adoption of computers for business in the Information Age, the time required to double the number of critical records is decreasing rapidly. At the current rate, the number of records will double in 5 years, and double again less than 3 years later. If the number of records continues to grow at the same rate of growth as that of the human population, the numbers are staggering; simple math tells us that *within 10 years, the number of records produced on the planet could be doubling every 60 minutes.*" Rich Lysakowski and Zahava Leibowitz, *Titanic 2020: A Call to Action.*

British Columbia discussed above. The second phase of the UBC Project was intended to address the long-term preservation of *inactive* electronic records. According to the project background document, "The immense scope and ubiquity of the issues surrounding the long-term preservation of authentic electronic records made evident the need for an interdisciplinary, international approach."

Led by the "International Team," the InterPARES Project is composed of several national and multinational research teams (Canadian, American, European, Italian, Australian, Asian, and The Collaborative Electronic Notebook Systems Assocation [CENSA]). These research teams are responsible for coordinating researchers, research partners, and related activities within their jurisdictions. Major funding has come from Canada's Social Science and Humanities Research Council, the U.S. National Historical Publications and Records Commission, and the Italian National Research Council.

The goal of the InterPARES Project is "to develop the theoretical and methodological knowledge essential to the permanent preservation of electronically generated records and, on the basis of this knowledge, to formulate model strategies, policies and standards capable of ensuring their preservation."

To meet this goal, the project's research plan has been divided into four interrelated domains of investigation and their respective research questions.

DOMAIN I: CONCEPTUAL REQUIREMENTS FOR PRESERVING AUTHENTIC ELECTRONIC RECORDS

1. What are the elements that all electronic records share?
2. What are the elements that allow us to differentiate among different types of electronic records?
3. Which of those elements will permit us to verify their authenticity over time?
4. Are the elements for verifying authenticity over time the same as those that permit us to verify their authenticity in time (i.e., at the point at which they were originally used)?
5. Can those elements be removed from where they are currently found to a place where they can more easily be preserved and still maintain the same validity?

DOMAIN II: APPRAISAL CRITERIA AND METHODOLOGY FOR AUTHENTIC ELECTRONIC RECORDS

1. What is the influence of digital technology on appraisal criteria?
2. How does appraisal differ according to the type of systems prevalent in each phase of computing?
3. How do the media and physical form of the records influence appraisal?
4. How do retrievability, intelligibility, functionality, and research needs influence appraisal?
5. Should restraints be imposed on the modification of systems at the time of appraisal?
6. Does the life cycle of electronic records differ from that for traditional records?
7. When in the course of their existence should electronic records be appraised?
8. Should electronic records be appraised more than once in the course of their existence and, if so, when?
9. How are electronic records scheduled?
10. Who should be responsible for appraising electronic records?
11. What are the appraisal criteria and methods for authentic electronic records?

DOMAIN III: METHODOLOGIES FOR PRESERVING AUTHENTIC ELECTRONIC RECORDS

1. What methods, procedures, and rules of long-term preservation are in use or being developed?
2. What are the procedural methods of authentication for preserved electronic records?
3. What are the technical methods of authentication for preserved electronic records?
4. What are the principles and criteria for media and storage management that are required for the preservation of authentic electronic records?
5. What are the responsibilities for the long-term preservation of authentic electronic records?

DOMAIN IV: A FRAMEWORK FOR DEVELOPING POLICIES, STRATEGIES, AND STANDARDS

1. What principles should guide the formulation of policies, strategies, and standards related to the long-term preservation of authentic electronic records?
2. What should be the criteria for developing national policies, strategies, and standards?
3. What should be the criteria for developing organizational policies, strategies, and standards?

This is a very ambitious research agenda, to say the least. The InterPARES Team has met six times (June and October 1998; March, June, and October 1999; and February 2000) to assign research responsibilities and review draft reports. The best summary of work to date is found in the text of various presentations by team members.[21] Anyone interested in preserving digital information will need to follow closely the work of the InterPARES project.

CONCLUSION

The above research projects provide the intellectual context for the day-to-day decisions that archivists and preservation administrators need to make about digital information. This research reminds us that our preservation efforts are complex, long-term strategies requiring both theoretical and practical components. The next chapter turns to the second part of the equation, the practical component, by discussing the preservation of physical media and file formats and summarizing a number of best practices in the preservation area.

NOTES

1. For more on the project, see University of British Columbia, *The Preservation of the Integrity of Electronic* Records, available at *www.slais.ubc.ca/users/duranti/intro.htm*. Page updated 1997.

2. In the words of the project team, "Diplomatics is a body of concepts and methods, originally developed in the seventeenth and eighteenth centuries, 'for the purpose of proving the reliability and authenticity of documents.' Over the centuries it has evolved 'into a very sophisticated system of ideas about the nature of records, their genesis and composition, their relationships with the actions and persons connected to them, and with their organizational, social and legal context.'" Available: *www.slais.ubc.ca/users/duranti/intro.htm*.

3. "Whereas diplomatics studies records as individual entities, 'archival science studies them as aggregations, analyzes their documentary and functional interrelationships, and studies the ways in which the records with all their relations can be controlled and communicated.'" Available: *www.slais.ubc.ca/users/duranti/intro.htm*.

4. A reliable record is "a record endowed with trustworthiness. Specifically, trustworthiness is conferred to a record by its degree of completeness and the degree of control on its creation procedure and/or its author's reliability." See "Template 3: What Is a Reliable Record in the Traditional Environment?" at *www.slais.ubc.ca/users/duranti/tem3.htm*.

5. An authentic record is one "whose genuineness can be established. . . . While a reliable record is one whose content you can trust, an authentic record is one whose provenance you can believe." See "Template 4: What Is an Authentic Record in the Traditional Environment?" at *www.slais.ubc.ca/users/duranti/tem4.htm*.

6. A good place to begin a review of the standard is at the home page of the Department of Defense's Joint Interoperability Test Command, which is administering the certification testing program for Records Management Applications: *jitc.fhu.disa.mil/recmgt/*.

7. For the text of the act, see *www.law.upenn.edu/bll/ulc/uecicta/uetast84.htm*.

8. There is much more of interest in the UETA, including sections on: notarization and acknowledgment; automated transactions; time and place of sending and receipt; transferable records; acceptance and distribution of electronic records by governmental agencies; and interoperability.

9. Richard C. Cox, "Electronic Systems and Records Management in the Information Age: An Introduction," *Bulletin of the American Society for Information Science* 23:5 (June/July 1997), 8. This entire issue focuses on electronic recordkeeping issues. For a summary of the research on warrants, see Wendy M. Duff's article, "Compiling Warrant in Support of the Functional Requirements for Recordkeeping," pages 12-13 of the same issue.

10. The full version can be found in *Bulletin of the American Society for Information Science* 23:5 (June/July 1997), 10–11. It is also found at the University of Pittsburgh's Web site: *www.lis.pitt.edu/~nhprc/meta96.html*.

11. For example, see Mark D. Giguere, "Automating Electronic Records Management in a Transactional Environment: The Philadelphia Story," *Bulletin of the American Society for Information Science* 23:5 (June/July 1997), 17-19. The Philadelphia Web site is: *www.phila.gov/city/departments/erms/erm.html*. A second test took place at Indiana University. See: Phillip Bantin, "NHPRC Project at the University of Indiana," *Bulletin of the American Society for Information Science* 23:5 (June/July 1997), 24. The Indiana Web site is: *www.indiana.edu/~libarche/index.html*. For a third test, see Alan Kowlowitz and Kristine Kelly, "Models for Action: Developing Practical Approaches to Electronic Records Management and Preservation," *Bulletin of the American Society for Information Science* 23:5 (June/July 1997), 20-24. This and other collaborative projects between the New York State Archives and the Center for Technology in Government (CTG) at the State University of New York at Albany can be found on the CTG Web site: *www.ctg.albany.edu*.

12. For information on the project, see: *info.wgbh.org/upf*.

13. Jeff Rothenberg, *Avoiding Technological Quicksand: Finding a Viable Technical Foundation for Digital Preservation* (Washington, DC: Council on Library and Information Resources, 1999).

14. Rothenberg, *Avoiding Technological Quicksand*, 1.

15. Rothenberg, *Avoiding Technological Quicksand*, 16.

16. Rothenberg, *Avoiding Technological Quicksand*, 30.

17. The Digital Library Federation (DLF, originally known as the National Digital Library Federation) exists under the organizational umbrella of the Council on Library and Information Resources (CLIR), which also incorporates the Commission on Preservation and Access. DLF was founded by 12 university research libraries and the Library of Congress, the National Archives and Records Administration, New York Public Library, and the Commission on Preservation and Access. The founding university libraries are California-Berkeley, Columbia, Cornell, Emory, Harvard, Michigan, Pennsylvania State, Princeton, South-

ern California, Stanford, Tennessee-Knoxville, and Yale. Eight additional university libraries have since joined the Federation: Carnegie-Mellon, Chicago, Indiana, Minnesota, North Carolina State, Pennsylvania, Texas-Austin, and the California Digital Library. See "Digital Library Federation: Organization," available online at *www.clir.org/diglib/dlforg.htm*. Page updated May 15, 1998.

18. The publications are: Caroline Arms (with Judith Klavans and Don Waters), *Enabling Access: A Report on a Workshop on Access Management* (Washington, DC: Digital Library Federation, Council on Library and Information Resources, 1999); and Ann Green (with JoAnn Dionne and Martin Dennis), *Preserving the Whole: A Two-Track Approach to Rescuing Social Science Data and Metadata* (Washington, DC: Digital Library Federation, Council on Library and Information Resources, 1999).

19. For a summary of the initiatives see: *www.clir.org/diglib/dlfinit.htm.*

20. Information about the InterPARES Project can be found at *www.interpares.org.*

21. See *www.interpares.org/whatsnew/conferences99.htm.*

4 STORAGE, HANDLING, AND PRESERVATION BEST PRACTICES

Not only have the last few years seen advances in theory about electronic records and digital preservation, they also have witnessed the codification of storage, handling, and other preservation practices. With both physical media and file formats, we now have guidelines to follow based upon the experience of many organizations.

But even with guidelines, preserving digital information is a complex matter. Jeff Rothenberg has proposed dealing with the complexity by focusing on triage in digital preservation. As he sees it, preservation has different imperatives in each of three different time frames:

- *Short Term.* Many organizations are faced with an "urgent need" to save digital material that is in imminent danger of becoming unreadable or inaccessible; some of these records already are difficult to access. These short-term "heroic efforts," however, may not be generalizable to new problems in the future.
- *Medium Term.* Organizations must quickly implement policies and technical procedures to prevent digital records from becoming vulnerable to imminent loss in the near future. The object is to keep today's digital records from being lost as formats and media evolve over the next few years.
- *Long Term.* As a society, we must develop solutions that do not require "continual heroic effort or repeated invention of new approaches every time formats, software or hardware paradigms, document types, or recordkeeping practices change." Such an approach must handle current and future records of unknown type in a uniform way while being capable of evolving as necessary.[1]

The focus of this chapter will be on the first two options, since the third scenario will be beyond the means and time frame of most organizations—except those who are the recognized leaders in the preservation or computing communities. Long-term solutions are most likely to emerge from the research initiatives discussed in Chapter 3.

This chapter covers the following topics:

- Deterioration of magnetic media
- Recommended storage
- Proper care and handling
- Other preservation best practices

"Digital documents last forever—or five years, whichever comes first." Jeff Rothenberg, *Avoiding Technological Quicksand: Finding a Viable Technical Foundation for Digital Preservation.*

DETERIORATION OF MAGNETIC MEDIA

As discussed in Chapter 2, magnetic media are composed of several layers: magnetic recording material, substrate, and binder. Each of these layers has its own preservation challenge.[2]

MAGNETIC PARTICLE INSTABILITIES

Magnetic particle store recorded information as changes in a magnetic field. Magnetic particles differ in stability—some particles retain their magnetic properties longer than others do. As a result, some tapes will retain magnetically-stored information longer than others.

There is not much that the preservation administrator can do to *prevent* deterioration—it is simply a fact of life that flows from the physical properties of the medium. However, we can slow the *rate* of deterioration by storing magnetic media in cooler temperatures. The humidity level does not have as much of an effect on the deterioration of the magnetic particles, though humidity will be important with some of the other layers.

SUBSTRATE DEFORMATION

The tape backing, or substrate, serves as a carrier for the magnetic layer. The substrate of modern tapes is made of polyester film, which is chemically stable and resistant to oxidation and hydrolysis.[3] The problem, however, is that stress, aging, and improper rewinding can lead to distortions and mistracking when the tapes are played.

The best way to minimize deformation is to store tapes in constant temperature and humidity. As the temperature and humidity change, the tape pack expands and contracts, which can lead to distortion.

Audio tapes and movie films from the 1940s and 1950s used a different backing material: acetate (cellulose acetate or cellulose triacetate), which is not as stable as polyester film and is subject to hydrolysis. Deteriorating acetate film is indicated by "vinegar syndrome," where a faint odor of vinegar (acetic acid) can be detected. Once tapes exhibit vinegar syndrome they can deteriorate very quickly, so immediate recopying is in order.

BINDER DEGRADATION

The binder holds the magnetic particles on the tape and facilitates tape transport. If the binder loses integrity, the tape may become unplayable. The binder is particularly subject to hydrolysis, in which molecules break down in the presence of water and lose stability and strength. As one would expect, high humidity encourages hydrolysis.

"The archival problems begin with the furtive nature of digital data storage itself. Paper may crumble, but its condition is usually obvious based upon its appearance. But for a typical disk or tape, short of running it in the proper computer, there is no easy way to determine whether it holds data or whether the information is deteriorating."—Stephen Manes, "Time and Technology Threaten Digital Archives."

Binder hydrolysis can lead to something called "sticky tape phenomenon." This is characterized by a softer than normal binder coating, higher friction, and gummy tape surface residue. The binder can also suffer a loss of lubricants, which can lead to additional tape reading errors.

OPTICAL MEDIA

Optical media are relatively less vulnerable than magnetic media. However, the recording material of optical media still are susceptible to degradation from prolonged exposure to high temperature and humidity (see Chapter 2). In the words of Charles M. Dollar, "In addition, the binder that holds the recording material to the polycarbonate substrate is subject to hydrolysis when exposed to high humidity, which can lead to small particles of the recording material separating from the substrate."[4]

RECOMMENDED STORAGE

As noted above, storage conditions can have a dramatic effect upon the longevity of magnetic media. According to John Van Bogart:

> Storing magnetic tape in a clean, controlled environment is the most important precaution you can take to extend the life of the media. High temperatures, high humidity, and the presence of dust and corrosive elements in the air all affect the physical components that make up magnetic tape and can result in loss of readable data through decreased magnetic capability and deterioration of the binder or backing of the tape. Too low temperature should also be avoided. In some cases, temperatures lower than 32 degrees Fahrenheit may actually harm the media and shorten rather than extend, life expectancies by risking exudation of the lubricant from the binder, which may clog heads. Rapid temperature changes are also undesirable as they introduce stresses in the wound tape pack. Tapes that are to be played in an environment different from the storage environment should be allowed to acclimate to the new temperature.[5]

In terms of temperature and humidity targets, the National Media Laboratory (NML) provides the ranges established by the U.S. National Archives:

"Like the Titanic, current computer systems are in part a result of [our] unwillingness to recognize and address the shortcomings of an industry that has mushroomed both technologically and financially. If this problem is not addressed now, in approximately 20 years, the Titanic may be replaced with a new icon of disaster."
Rich Lysakowski and Zahava Leibowitz, *Titanic 2020: A Call to Action.*

- *Temperature:* 65 degrees Fahrenheit plus or minus three degrees
- *Relative Humidity:* 40% plus or minus 5%

NML notes, however, that there really are *two* storage environments, one for "access storage" and the other for "archival storage." Each environment has a different purpose and, hence, different temperature and humidity targets. These differences are summarized in Table 4.1.[6]

Table 4.1 reinforces the fact that any preservation administrator must first determine *what* he or she is trying to accomplish before turning to the *how* of an implementation plan. A common strategy with digital media is to have more than one copy of a record: a preservation copy in archival storage and a use copy in access storage. This also provides security in case of a natural or other disaster.

Table 4.1 Access and Archival Storage

Key Feature	Access Storage	Archival Storage
Function	To provide storage for media that allow immediate access and playback	To provide storage that preserves the media for as long as possible
Acclimation required prior to playback?	No	Yes
Media Life Expectancy	At least 10 years when stored at the indicated temperature and humidity conditions	The maximum allowed for the particular media type
Temperature Set Point	At or near room ambient. In the range of 60° to 74° Fahrenheit	Significantly lower than room ambient. As low as 40° Fahrenheit
Humidity Set Point	At or near room ambient. In the range of 25 to 55% relative humidity	Significantly lower than room ambient. As low as 20% relative humidity
Temperature Variations	Difference between maximum and minimum value should not exceed 7° Fahrenheit	Difference between maximum and minimum value should not exceed 7° Fahrenheit
Humidity Variations	Difference between maximum and minimum value should not exceed 20% relative humidity	Difference between maximum and minimum value should not exceed 10% relative humidity

To summarize the key points about storage conditions:

- Lower temperature slows the rate of decomposition.
- Lower humidity reduces binder hydrolysis (tape) and corrosion (tape/optical disk).
- Stable temperature and humidity reduce stress on the media.
- Removing dust and debris can prevent them from getting wound into the tape pack causing loss of signal.
- Controlling pollutants can reduce corrosive gases and their harmful effects.

PROPER CARE AND HANDLING

Appropriate storage is necessary but not sufficient for digital preservation. The way we care for and handle the media also can do much to preserve the items and the information they contain.

Before discussing detailed guidelines for care and handling, it is important to clear up some confusion in terms. Charles Dollar, in a recently published book, tried to clarify the differences among four terms for media renewal that are often incorrectly used interchangeably: reformat, copy, convert, and migrate.[7]

- *Reformatting* of electronic records means that there is a change to the underlying bit stream, but there is no change in the representation or intellectual content of the records. Typically, reformatting is associated with the transfer of a bit stream from one storage medium to a different one. For example, moving from 9-track tape to cassette would be reformatting, as would be transforming records from EDCDIC (the coding used on mainframe computers) to ASCII (the coding used on personal computers).
- *Copying* electronic records means transferring them from old storage media to new storage media with the same format specifications and without any loss in structure, content, or context. In copying electronic records the underlying bit stream pattern on one storage medium is replicated on a new but identical, storage medium (e.g., 3480 tape to 3480 tape).
- *Converting* electronic records involves their export or import from one software environment to another without the loss of structure, content, or context even though the underlying bit stream is likely to be altered. Conversion occurs when electronic records are moved from one software environment or applica-

"Human carelessness and maliciousness, always threats to preservation of a document, may be even more dangerous for electronic products. How can we be certain which is the authentic version? There are no standards yet in place for maintaining digital information or for recording the incremental changes that are inserted because the technology enables the delivery of fluid documents."—Linda Beebe and Barbara Meyers, "The Unsettled State of Archiving."

tion to another, for example, converting a file from WordPerfect to Microsoft Word.

- *Migrating* electronic records usually involves moving them from proprietary legacy systems that lack software functionality to open systems. Currently the only way to migrate the records and their essential software functionality is to write special programs. For example, if an archivist found old magnetic tapes in storage that came from an obsolete computer system, the only way to read the data would be to write a special program. This is more complex than is generally thought, especially since archivists must preserve the integrity of the records during the migration.

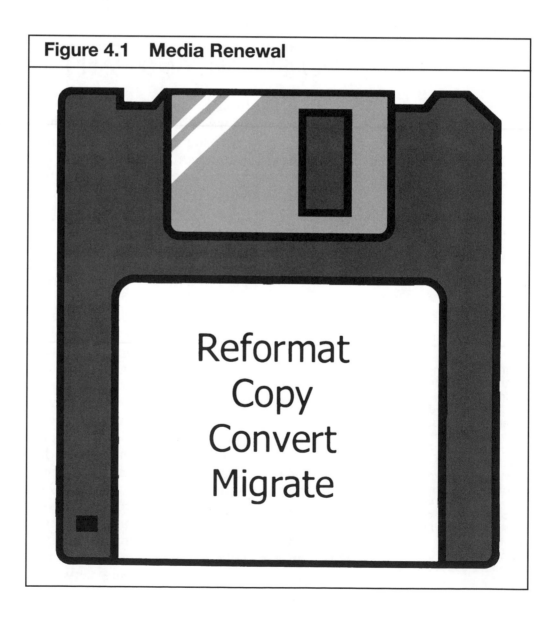

Figure 4.1   Media Renewal

Reformat
Copy
Convert
Migrate

With these terms clarified, we now can turn to specific recommended practices for the handling of physical media. These practices are excerpted from the "Guide to the Care and Handling of Magnetic Tape," issued by Ampex Corporation.[8] These are the major recommendations:

- Tape should be handled only in no smoking, no food, clean areas.
- Do not let tape or leader ends trail on the floor.
- Do not drop or subject tape to sudden shock.
- Keep tape away from magnetic fields.
- Tape storage areas should be cool and dry. Never leave open reels of cassette tapes exposed to the sun.
- Store open reel and cassette tapes with the reels or tape packs vertical. Reels should be supported by the hub. Tapes should be stored like books on a library shelf—on end. They should not be stored laying flat.
- Use high quality reels or cassettes, boxes and containers, and accessories.
- Return tapes to their containers when they are not in use.
- Do not use general purpose adhesive tape to secure the tape end or for splicing.
- Minimize tape handling.
- Do not touch the tape surface or the edge of the tape pack unless absolutely necessary, and then wear lint-free gloves.
- Clean the tape path thoroughly at recommended intervals.
- Ensure tapes to be reused are thoroughly erased before they are put back into service.
- Avoid contact with water.
- Do not store tapes on radiators, window sills, electronic equipment, or machinery.
- If shipping tapes, be certain that all of the above practices are followed.

In addition to these general recommendations, there are two other tape handling considerations unique to a preservation environment. The first involves periodic "retensioning" or "rewinding" to redistribute mechanical stress as well as to prevent wrinkling and tape deformation. An accepted practice is to rewind open-reel tapes held in long-term storage every three years. Cassettes and cartridges, however, usually do not require rewinding.

The second preservation practice is a regular monitoring and inspection program. The purpose of the inspection program is to identify problems with the fragile media before there is a catastrophic loss or failure. This is done by selecting an annual statistical sample of the collection. The U.S. National Archives has issued the following guidelines for selecting a sample:

- Select all storage media annually if there are fewer than fifty.
- Select a 20% random sample of the storage media when the total number of storage media ranges between 50 and 1800.
- Select a random sample of 384 storage media when the total number of storage media is 1,801 or greater.[9]

This final step of inspecting storage media is one that organizations often overlook. It is essential, however, that this loose end be tied up in order to have a complete preservation program.

PRESERVATION FILE FORMATS

Choosing a stable file format is another important preservation consideration. As noted in Chapter 2, for each type of digital information we encounter—text, image, sound, or video—there are low-level formats that are likely to remain supported, at least for the foreseeable future. For example, word processing documents can be saved as an ASCII file, a standard for text files that can be read using almost any software. The disadvantage of an ASCII file, however, is that formatting is lost (different sized fonts, bold, italics, etc.). By definition, proprietary, "leading edge" solutions always will have features that go beyond those found in the universally-accepted standards. A second reality is that saving a file from a proprietary to a standard file format often leads to a loss of features and functionality.

Many organizations, however, are turning to formats popular on the World Wide Web in the hope that these formats will survive. This hope is based upon the large installed base of the formats and the support offered by a number of vendors. There are three principal formats:

- HTML (Hypertext Markup Language)
- XML (Extensible Markup Language)
- PDF (Portable Document Format)

HTML

HTML is the "markup language" used on the World Wide Web. Using HTML, we can display a "page" using various browsers or readers. The advantage of HTML is its wide availability and potential for ongoing support. For long-term preservation, however, newer formats include features that will better fix the content in time and provide descriptive elements linked to the documents.

XML

Extensible Markup Language is a universal format for structured documents and data. Structured documents include such things as spreadsheets, address books, technical drawings, etc. Programs that produce such data store them on disk, either in a binary or text format. A text format would allow one, if necessary, to look at the data without using the program that produced it. In the words of the World Wide Web Consortium, "XML is a set of rules, guidelines, conventions, whatever you want to call them, for designing text formats for such data, in a way that produces files that are easy to generate and read (by a computer), that are unambiguous, and that avoid common pitfalls, such as lack of extensibility, lack of support for internationalization/localization, and platform dependency." XML is license-free, platform-independent and well-supported.[10]

Many involved in digital preservation view XML as our best hope for combining document content and descriptive information in one unit that can be read by future software packages.[11]

PDF

Adobe Portable Document Format (PDF) is the open de facto standard for electronic document distribution worldwide. Adobe PDF is a universal file format that preserves all of the fonts, formatting, colors, and graphics of any source document, regardless of the application and the platform used to create it. PDF files can be shared, viewed, navigated, and printed exactly as intended by anyone with a free reader. Any document, even scanned paper, can be converted to Adobe PDF.[12]

Though PDF was developed by one vendor and, technically, is "proprietary," its open nature and large market presence makes it an attractive option for medium-term if not long-term storage. Many institutional settings, particularly court systems, are adopting PDF for the submission and storage of electronic documents.

FORMAT SUMMARY

Table 4.2 summarizes the advantages and disadvantages of these three popular formats:[13]

Table 4.2 Advantages and Disadvantages of HTML, XML, and PDF

Format	Advantages	Disadvantages	Most Common Usage
HTML	• Wide platform support, can be viewed in any browser • Good for delivering simple text • Conversion-to-HTML tools getting better	• Viewing inconsistencies among browsers • Some features not available in early version browsers • Limited authoring tools • Lacks "document" concept • Can't save or print files with fidelity information	• Delivery of static information • Output from other systems (such as databases)
XML	• Stores content as well as context (metadata) • Can display dynamic information as a document • XSL (Extensible Style Sheet) could allow for more control over presentation	• Emerging standard • Limited tools for authoring and viewing • Presentation standard still in progress • Limited industry expertise	• Delivery of dynamic data • Business-to-business e-commerce (purchase orders, invoices)
PDF	• Complete visual integrity (layouts, fonts, colors, pagination) • Platform and application independent • Free "reader" plug-in with extensive search and navigation features • Optimized file compression and delivery • Exact correlation between on-screen and printed output • Ability to recreate paper documents into searchable, viewable electronic files	• Users need to install free Acrobat Reader • Output from some electronic sources may be a problem	• Delivery of visually rich content (marketing materials, published information and documents originating from paper)

To summarize, there are four keys to maximizing the longevity of digital information: (1) choose the most stable technology possible, (2) choose the most stable format possible, (3) store the records in the best possible environment, and (4) implement proper care and handling procedures.

OTHER PRESERVATION BEST PRACTICES

In recent years there have been a number of attempts to summarize best practices in digital preservation. These summaries usually are intended for specific audiences or constituencies of various kinds and provide many useful ideas for the person new to a preservation program. This section discusses best practices issued by the following:

- European Union
- State of New York
- Australian Archives
- Victoria Public Records Office

EUROPEAN UNION

In 1996, the DLM Forum was organized jointly by the Member States of the European Union and the European Commission in Brussels. The forum brought together experts from industry, research, administration, and archives to discuss the memory of the information society. The principal outcome of the DLM Forum was a publication, *Guidelines on Best Practices for Using Electronic Information: How to Deal with Machine-Readable Data and Electronic Documents.*[14]

One of the most interesting features of the DLM *Guidelines* is the use of a "traffic signal" approach to identify how far one can rely on particular standards: a "green light" means that a standard is stable and recognized; an "amber light" means that the standard is pending or used only by a few suppliers; and a "red light" means that the standard is proprietary and not guaranteed to last. This makes it very easy for someone to sort through the maze of items that are called standards.

The *Guidelines* also are very good on clarifying the two main ways of structuring information, databases and documents. With a database, data are placed in a "pool" of information from which they can be retrieved and updated. Databases pose problems when it comes to accessing data a long time after the normal lifetime of the database. In these cases there are two common options:

"Those of us concerned with the preservation of information and knowledge must not forget that our mission is without journey's end." Harold Billings, "The Information ARK: Selection Issues in the Preservation Process," *Wilson Library Bulletin* (April 1994), 35.

- Copying the database to a lower-level format, such as plain text. This solution may lead to the loss of some elements of the database.
- Keeping the application program that generated the database, including the documentation. This solution often means keeping not just the application but also the computer system on which it runs.

"A record remains useful only as long as the medium on which its information is stored can be read and understood. There are many examples of historical records that were preserved but became unusable because the ability to read them was lost. Ancient Egyptian hieroglyphics were undecipherable for centuries until the discovery of the Rosetta Stone in 1799." United States Congress, House Committee on Government Operations, *Taking a Byte out of History: The Archival Preservation of Federal Computer Records.*

In many cases the database is fully integrated into a proprietary application. Preserving a database is complicated by the lack of standard formats to guarantee long-term accessibility.

The second way to structure information, the document, is used when data are arranged in an ordered fashion to present an argument or describe an activity. Documents come in many different forms—letters, notes, memos, forms, reports, etc.—each of which require special treatment. Documents often are grouped together to form coherent units of information. Classification of documents is an important factor on finding information easily.

A particular challenge to archivists and preservation administrators is that fact that both types of structured information (databases and documents) are increasingly combined in one record. An example would be an e-mail message with attachments or a word-processing document that is dynamically linked to a database. Such compound records present unique preservation challenges.

The DLM *Guidelines* list the four stages in an organization's transition from paper to electronic documents:

1. The traditional office, based on paper documents
2. A mixed office with documents on paper and in electronic form
3. The conversion of paper documents by scanning
4. An entirely electronic office, where all documents are produced, received, and distributed electronically.

At this point in our organizations, we are mainly dealing with the second and third stages. We are trying to sort out the relationships between digital and nondigital documents and are trying to determine strategies for long-term access to information.

One specific suggestion in the *Guidelines* is that a major criterion for evaluating products should be the degree to which they are based on stable and open standards. They recommend including the following clause in all procurement documents: "To guarantee preservation of the awarding organization's data and long-term access, the supplier undertakes to provide all the hardware, software and documen-

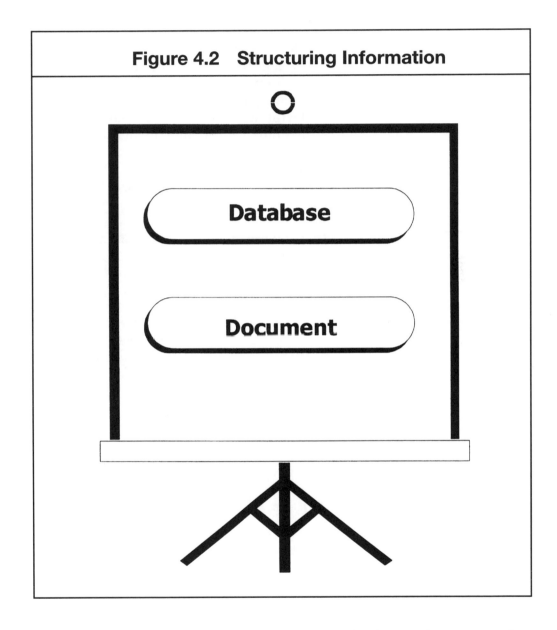

Figure 4.2 Structuring Information

Database

Document

tation necessary to recover data generated by his applications and to export them to other environments and other formats."[15]

The *Guidelines* strongly recommend that a global strategy be defined at the outset of any project to ensure that everyone is involved. A multidisciplinary team should be established to define and monitor the strategy. Among the responsibilities of the team could be the following:

- Taking account of users' requirements (including legal aspects);
- Identifying important records;
- Defining rules for an efficient classification plan;

- Defining standards and specifications to ensure the independence of data from media and to guarantee their durability;
- Defining an appraisal scheme;
- Identifying those responsible for each task in the life cycle;
- Defining a training and awareness policy;
- Monitoring the implementation of the new system.[16]

In addition to its recommendations on planning, the DLM *Guidelines* offer numerous best practices in the area of implementation. These are some of the suggestions:

- Each document or database must be clearly identified by the organization responsible for electronic information management.
- Background documentation should be provided for all electronic information. It is then kept by the person responsible for electronic information management at each stage in the life cycle.
- No data should be destroyed or changed without an approval procedure. This ensures that the context is preserved.
- When electronic information is converted from one format to another, care has to be taken to avoid accidental loss of data. Proprietary formats do not always convert seamlessly.

The DLM Forum has done an admirable job of compiling best practices for the use of both the European Community and the rest of the world. Anyone designing a program to preserve digital information would do well to consult these guidelines.

STATE OF NEW YORK

The State of New York received a grant from the National Historical Publications and Records Commission (NHPRC) in 1996 to conduct a project called "Models for Action: Developing Practical Approaches to Electronic Records Management and Preservation." The project was a collaboration among the New York State Archives and Records Administration (SARA), the Center for Technology in Government (CTG), the State University of New York at Albany, the New York State Adirondack Park Agency, the New York State Forum for Information Resource Management, and eight corporate partners led by Intergraph Corporation.[17]

The project integrated practical and theoretical work in electronic records management with network-based system development methodologies and business process improvement practices. The goal of the project was to develop practical tools for use by state government agencies and other entities.

A major project result was the publication in January 1999 of *Practical Tools for Electronic Records Management and Preservation*.[18]

This publication tried to bridge the gap between theory and practice by presenting generalizable tools that link records management practices to business objectives. The tools can be used by any organization to:

- bring the record to the forefront of system design activities.
- identify electronic records functionality as part of system design.
- create electronic records that support legal and evidentiary needs.
- create electronic records that are accessible and usable over time.
- integrate diverse document forms and formats into records.
- identify the need for internal and external primary and secondary access to records.

The New York State project began with the following definition: A "record" is the complete set of documentation required to provide evidence of a business transaction. The team then defined three functional requirements for electronic records management and preservation that were based upon the research conducted at the University of Pittsburgh (see Chapter 3). The final New York State functional requirements are:

1. *Records Capture.* Records are created or captured and identified to support the business process and meet all records management requirements related to the process.
2. *Records Maintenance and Accessibility.* Electronic records are maintained so that they are accessible and retain their integrity for as long as they are needed.
3. *System Reliability.* A system is administered in accordance with best practices in the information resource management (IRM) field to ensure the reliability of the records it produces.

In order to translate these requirements into action, the team developed a "Records Requirement Analysis and Implementation Tool" (RRAIT). This tool supports the identification of records management requirements as well as the strategies for their implementation. The RRAIT is composed of two parts: the "Records Requirement Elicitation Component" (RREC) and the "Records Requirement Implementation Component" (RRIC). Taken together, the components facilitate the identification and implementation of application-specific records management requirements.[19]

The Records Requirement Elicitation Component facilitates the identification of records management requirements during business-process improvement and systems-analysis activities. It is divided into three levels:

1. *Business Process Level.* Focuses on records management requirements associated with the business process that is to be automated.
2. *Record Level.* Captures records management requirements associated with access and use over time, for both the record in aggregate and its component parts.
3. *System Level.* Focuses on how, from a technical standpoint, the information system will accommodate the integration of, and ongoing access to, record components.

The Records Requirements Implementation Component supports the identification of management, policy, and technology strategies that address the requirements once they have been identified by the three levels of the RREC. The RRIC also has three levels: management strategies, policy strategies, and technology strategies. The project report also contains charts, templates, and implementation examples. Finally, the report gives six guidelines for use of the tools:

1. An organization must first recognize the importance of its business records and the costs and risks associated with ignoring them.
2. The degree to which the tools are effective depends upon the organization's readiness and willingness to change.
3. One of the most critical factors for effective use of the tools is getting the appropriate people to answer the questions.
4. The tools help organizations identify the functionality that is required in a system to support records management requirements.
5. Several methods can be used to answer the questions in the RRAIT.
6. Technology awareness activities should be conducted in conjunction with the use of the tools.

The Models for Action project offers an excellent practical tool for implementing recent electronic records research. This is an important beginning point for anyone who finds him- or herself faced with the task of integrating preservation considerations into the design of new information systems.

AUSTRALIAN ARCHIVES

The Australian Archives has been one of the leaders in the management of electronic records. In particular, its technical publications have been recognized worldwide for the soundness of their approach and the usefulness of their advice. In terms of best practices, two publications are worthy of special mention: *Managing Electronic Records: A*

> "Efforts to preserve physical media . . . provide only a short-term, partial solution to the general problem of preserving digital information. Indeed, technological obsolescence represents a far greater threat to information in digital form than the inherent physical fragility of many digital media." John Garrett and Donald Waters, *Preserving Digital Information: Report of the Task Force on Archiving Digital Information.*

Shared Responsibility and *Keeping Electronic Records: Policy for Electronic Recordkeeping in the Commonwealth Government.*

Managing Electronic Records was released in 1995 and revised in 1997.[20] The document was designed to contain the essential elements of the Australian Archives' strategy for the management of electronic records. The Archives emphasizes the management of records from the time of their creation, forming one records continuum. Their experience has shown that the successful management of electronic records "requires involvement right from records creation and systems development." The essential features of such an approach involve:

- Strategic management of electronic records;
- The development and implementation of electronic record-keeping systems;
- The migration of electronic records, with their content, structure, and context intact, across changes in software and hardware platforms.

The Australian Archives no longer defines records in terms of the physical objects that carry them. The new definition is as follows: "A record is that which is created and kept as *evidence* of agency or individual functions, activities and transactions. To be considered *evidence,* a record must possess content, structure and context and be part of a recordkeeping system."[21]

The archives then makes a strong statement about why early and active involvement with electronic records is necessary:

Records without context, structure or content are simply "noise"; unreadable disks are just plastic. If appropriate measures are not put in place, the rights and entitlements of citizens will be undermined and governments and administrations will find it increasingly difficult to operate effectively and to account for their actions.[22]

The "appropriate measures" involve a shared responsibility for electronic records. Originating agencies have the responsibility for maintaining electronic records and ensuring their accessibility over time. While the archives is in a position to manage some electronic records, it does not have the technology or resources to manage electronic records from all governmental systems. It will only take certain electronic records agreed upon in advance. The archives' role will primarily be one of advising agencies in the following ways:

- Identifying electronic records that are of enduring value.
- Disposing of electronic records that do not have enduring value.

- Identifying information or metadata that needs to be captured and maintained with electronic records of enduring value if they are to remain identifiable and accessible over time.
- Providing advice on access to archival electronic records.
- Assisting with the development of recordkeeping systems.

Appendix 1 of *Managing Electronic Records* is one of the finest summaries of best practices to be found anywhere.[23] It contains principles and strategies organized around four key areas of electronic records management and preservation:

1. Creating electronic records and capturing them into electronic recordkeeping systems.
2. Designing, building, and using electronic systems that keep records.
3. Maintaining and managing electronic records over time.
4. Making electronic records accessible.

The strategies and principles were developed by the Australian Council of Archives in conjunction with a variety of corporations, government agencies, archives, and records management sectors. The best practices are so important and have been so influential that they deserve reprinting in their entirety. The strategies and principles follow below.

Creating electronic records and capturing them into electronic recordkeeping systems.

Principles

1. Each organization's business processes and systems shall operate to capture records which provide evidence of its business activities conducted electronically.
2. Responsibility for creating and capturing records shall rest with individuals nominated as responsible at all levels of the organizational structure and with the organization as a whole

Strategies

1. Each organization should identify relevant and accountable recordkeeping requirements to determine what records are to be created or captured and how long they should be retained.
2. Each organization should determine, through risk assessment, the degree to which its different activities need to be supported by reliable and authentic records.

3. Each organization should define its own statement of the boundaries of business processes and systems, and the legal and other requirements that affect them, to facilitate the capture of business communications as records when entering or leaving the specified domain.
4. Archives institutions should establish documentation strategies focusing on organizational recordkeeping approaches.
5. Archives institutions should promote themselves to targeted records creators, demonstrating the benefits of documenting their work through electronic recordkeeping.

Designing, building and using electronic systems that keep records.

Principles

1. The major objectives of electronic recordkeeping systems shall be to manage the content, context and structure of records as a whole and to ensure that records are reliable and authentic.
2. Electronic recordkeeping systems shall facilitate the reuse of information contained within records while securely maintaining reliable and authentic records.
3. Each electronic recordkeeping system shall be designed to comply with relevant national and international standards and best practices.
4. Electronic recordkeeping systems shall provide one corporate interface to all records relating to a particular business activity, regardless of the media in which the records are created and kept.

Strategies

1. Each organization should identify recordkeeping requirements to be satisfied by electronic recordkeeping systems, including operational business needs, legal requirements, industry best practice and the expectations of society.
2. Each organization should determine whether its requirements should be satisfied by one or more than one electronic recordkeeping system.
3. Recordkeeping requirements may be satisfied through dedicated electronic recordkeeping systems or by designing and implementing recordkeeping functionality into systems not primarily designed for recordkeeping.
4. Electronic recordkeeping systems should operate to comply with . . . relevant standards.
5. Electronic recordkeeping systems should be regularly audited

for compliance against the specified recordkeeping requirements.

6. When implementing electronic recordkeeping systems, organizations should ensure that such systems are recognized and used as the authorized organizational recordkeeping system/s.

Maintaining and managing electronic records over time.

Principles

1. Electronic records shall be maintained for as long as they are needed.
2. Electronic records shall be maintained in electronic form.
3. Each organization shall maintain electronic records to ensure that the evidence is accessible, comprehensible and managed for as long as it is required.

Strategies

1. Each organization should migrate electronic records of continuing value through successive upgrades of hardware and software in such a way as to retain the full functionality of the preceding systems and the integrity of the electronic records created in them.
2. Each organization should use each such migration as an opportunity to re-appraise the decisions to retain or delete electronic records.
3. Appraisal should be undertaken rigorously at the time of designing the recordkeeping system or as early in the life of the records as is possible, to mitigate the need for continual migration of records.
4. Each organization should identify, capture, maintain, and migrate the metadata required for electronic records and the systems that create them, including contextual information about the records and the activities that they document, in conjunction with the records themselves.
5. The connection between the records and the metadata should be maintained for as long as the records, including through migration of hardware and software systems.
6. Each organization should identify and adopt relevant technological standards that will help ensure that electronic records will be available and usable for as long as they are required.
7. Each organization should determine who will maintain and manage its electronic records of continuing value in an envi-

ronment that is able to support the content, context and structure of the records over time. This may be the organization itself, an archives institution or another organization; that is, the custody of electronic records may be distributed, rather than in centralized archival custody. These decisions may be affected by external policy or other requirements.

8. Each organization should establish standards and procedures to ensure the integrity of its electronic records over time.
9. Electronic records management should employ sound data management techniques.
10. A variety of information management tools should be explored to facilitate the goals of electronic recordkeeping, including electronic management and workflow tools.

Making electronic records accessible.

Principles

1. Each organization shall aim to provide appropriate electronic access to records irrespective of their location, both within and beyond the boundaries of the organization.
2. Each organization shall protect its electronic records from inappropriate access.
3. Each organization shall be able to provide access to electronic records in ways that will present meaningful evidence of the business activity that they document, in addition to presenting their information content.

Strategies

1. Electronic recordkeeping systems implemented within organizations should facilitate appropriate remote electronic access to records by employees and authorized external users.
2. Archivists should work with custodians of electronic records to develop networked access systems that are available and easy to use, while protecting the custodian's operational systems from unauthorized access.
3. Governments and other organizations should consider the requirements for and provide access to electronic records in the development of information locator and "one stop shop" services and systems.
4. Archival information systems should serve as hubs for networked access beyond organizational boundaries.
5. Archival information systems should provide online finding

aids, standardized records searching and retrieval tools and compliance with access policies.

6. Archives institutions in partnership with other organizations should pursue opportunities to enhance access to electronic records, including value-added services, through entrepreneurial and cooperative ventures.

The second publication of the Australian Archives, *Keeping Electronic Records*, builds upon the foundation laid above.[24] First issued in 1995, *Keeping Electronic Records* focuses on maintaining accountability in the electronic age by preserving evidence of agency business transactions.

One key to this accountability is the use of "recordkeeping systems" rather than "information systems." Computer systems often are not designed to keep evidence of transactions carried out using them. In the words of *Keeping Electronic Records*, "Without this evidence your organization will lose its corporate memory, will face increasing difficulty in meetings its accountability requirements and the nation as a whole will lose significant portions of its archival heritage."

Furthermore, the computing environment most likely to maintain accessibility and authenticity will be found in the originating agency rather than an archives. It will be much too expensive for the archives to duplicate every possible configuration of hardware and software in the various agencies. As Commonwealth policy, original records will remain with the creating agency unless:

- The agency which created the records is about to be or has become defunct and no agency is identifiable as its successor to the function.
- The archives enters into an agreement with an agency to take custody of the electronic records.

One of the most useful parts of the Australian document for any preservation administrator is its listing of criteria for transfer of electronic records to an archives. While decisions will be made on a case-by-case basis, the Australian Archives considers the following factors to be key:

- The records have been appraised and have enduring value.
- The records have sufficient metadata and contextual information to meet the Archives' descriptive standards for electronic records.
- The resource impact is assessed and is manageable.
- The records proposed for transfer conform with media and formats supported by the Archives.

- The transferring agency will meet all processing requirements (including duplication) necessary for the records to meet the Archives' standards for transfer and access.

To summarize, this second Australian document provides excellent guidance for the archivist or preservation administrator considering a noncustodial option. The Australian Archives has been the worldwide leader in advocating and implementing this option.

VICTORIA PUBLIC RECORDS OFFICE

The Australian State of Victoria has issued one of the finest documents to date on the development and implementation of an electronic records strategy. The Victoria Public Records Office (PROV) developed the Victorian Electronic Records Strategy (VERS) in consultation with public and private partners. This excellent document should receive wider attention so it no longer remains Victoria's secret.[25]

As with most of the Australian work on electronic records and digital preservation, VERS draws heavily upon the University of Pittsburgh's functional requirements and the writings of David Bearman. The VERS project developed a test bed system to prototype a "future state" electronic document processing and records capture system. The prototype enabled the Victoria Public Records Office to develop and evaluate techniques for electronic records creation, management, and archiving.

The VERS team stated its conclusions in an unambiguous way that would surprise many people involved in preserving digital information:

- "Capture of electronic records into a long term format, with much of the contextual information captured automatically, is possible and achievable now."
- "Archiving of electronic records is possible and achievable now."

These conclusions arose from the team's work to develop a preferred long-term electronic record format and to specify a minimum metadata set that should be associated with every electronic record. PROV determined that an electronic record had to be "a fully documenting object." They chose to describe these objects in Extensible Markup Language (XML), a text-based standard. Furthermore, an electronic record had to be composed of one or more documents, contextual information relating this record with other records, and evidential integrity checks.

The PROV team also began with the belief that electronic records should be captured at the time of creation. They stated several "strong reasons" for this requirement:

- The record is more reliable as evidence if captured at the time of creation.
- There is more chance that the record will, in fact, be captured if it is done immediately.
- Information capture at the time of the original transaction is both cheaper and more reliable than later data entry.

At the heart of the project was the development of an "archival system demonstrator" and a "retrieval system demonstrator." Each was built as a separate system, partly to demonstrate that electronic records were self-contained and could be passed reliably between systems without further information. The solution also allowed implementation in various organizational settings:

- Central records custody or distributed records custody
- Highly routine environments amenable to workflow or environments that allow for *ad hoc* activity.

In brief, VERS moved from a theoretical analysis of digital preservation to a practical demonstration of an implementable solution through completion of process analysis, system construction, and demonstrations to stakeholders. The VERS report also has one of the most complete estimates of costs found anywhere in the literature on digital preservation. For this reason alone, the *Victorian Electronic Records Strategy Final Report* should be required reading for anyone undertaking a digital preservation initiative.

CONCLUSION

This chapter has summarized recent digital preservation writings in three areas: storage, handling, and organizational best practices. This has been a wide-ranging discussion that focused on some recognized and respected approaches to the problems discussed earlier in the book.

The next chapter turns to two types of digital information that have emerged in the last few years and that present particular preservation challenges: electronic mail and Web pages. What can we do to preserve digital information embodied in these two forms?

NOTES

1. Jeff Rothenberg, *Avoiding Technological Quicksand: Finding a Viable Technical Foundation for Digital Preservation* (Washington, DC: Council on Library and Information Resources, 1999), 5–6.

2. The following discussion is adapted from John W.C. Van Bogart, *Magnetic Tape Storage and Handling: A Guide for Libraries and Archives* (Washington, DC: Commission on Preservation and Access; St. Paul, MN: National Media Laboratory, 1995), 2–7. The National Media Laboratory in St. Paul has conducted extensive research into the deterioration of digital information. Though much of this *Guide* is directed at audio and video preservation, it is relevant to our discussion since computer tapes use the same underlying technologies.

3. In hydrolysis, long molecules are broken apart by a reaction with water to produce shorter molecules. The shorter molecules are not as strong as the longer molecules. See Van Bogart, *Magnetic Tape Storage and Handling*, 3–4.

4. Charles M. Dollar, *Authentic Electronic Records: Strategies for Long-Term Access* (Chicago: Cohasset Associates, 1999), 98.

5. Van Bogart, *Magnetic Tape Storage and Handling*, 14.

6. Van Bogart, *Magnetic Tape Storage and Handling*, 18.

7. Dollar, *Authentic Electronic Records*, 26–32, 59–72.

8. Ampex Recording Media Corporation, "Guide to the Care and Handling of Magnetic Tape," reprinted in Van Bogart, *Magnetic Tape Storage and Handling*, 23.

9. Dollar, *Authentic Electronic Records*, 99–100.

10. For additional information, see "XML in 10 Points" on the Web site of the World Wide Web Consortium: *www/w3.org/xml/1999/xml-in-10-points*.

11. See, for example, Reagan Moore, et al., "Collection-Based Persistent Digital Archives: Part 1," *D-Lib Magazine* 6:3 (March 2000), available at *www.dlib.org/dlib/march00/moore/03moore-pt1.html*.

12. For additional information, see the Adobe Web site, particularly *www.adobe.com/products/acrobat/adobepdf.html*.

13. The chart is taken from Joel C. Messenger, "Document Delivery on the Web," *Inform* 13:2 (February 1999), 13.

14. European Union, *Guidelines on Best Practices for Using Electronic Information: How to Deal with Machine-Readable Data and Electronic Documents*, Updated and enlarged ed. (Luxembourg: Office for Official Publications of the European Communities, 1997).

15. DLM *Guidelines,* 16.
16. DLM *Guidelines,* 20.
17. See *www.ctg.albany.edu/projects/er/ermn.html.*
18. State University of New York at Albany. *Practical Tools for Electronic Records Management and Preservation,* available at *www.ctg.albany.edu/resources/abstract/mfa-toolkit.html.* Page updated June 29, 1999.
19. The document is available at *www.ctg.albany.edu/resources/pdfrpwp/mfa_toolkit.pdf.*
20. Australian Archives, *Managing Electronic Records,* 1995, rev. 1997. Available at *www.naa.gov.au/techpub/manelrec/ManagingER.html.* A second technical publication from the Australian Archives also worth consulting is *Keeping Electronic Records: Policy for Electronic Recordkeeping in the Commonwealth Government,* available at *www.naa.gov.au/recordkeeping/er/keeping_er/intro.html.* Page updated March 30, 2000.
21. Australian Archives, *Managing Electronic Records.*
22. Australian Archives, *Managing Electronic Records.*
23. Available at *www.naa.gov.au/govserv/techpub/manelrec/merappendix1.htm.*
24. Available at *www.naa.gov.au/govserv/techpub/elecrecd/KeepingER.html.*
25. Public Records Office Victoria, *Victorian Electronic Records Strategy Final Report* (Victoria: Public Records Office of Victoria, 1998). Available online at *www.prov.vic.gov.au/VERS/.*

5 ELECTRONIC MAIL AND WEB PAGES

Preserving digital information always is a moving target: just when we think we have a solution in our sights, the target speeds up or changes direction. Two of the most recent accelerations or deviations involve electronic mail and Web pages. What special challenges do these systems present? What strategies can we use to preserve this digital information? Will current electronic records theory and practice apply in these contexts? Must we rethink what we do as archivists and preservation administrators?

ELECTRONIC MAIL (E-MAIL)

Before addressing preservation, it is important to define just what we mean by electronic mail. E-mail is a system that enables users to compose, transmit, receive and manage text and graphic electronic messages and images across networks and through gateways connecting other local area networks. This information consists primarily of messages, but may include attachments such as calendars, directories, distribution lists, word processing documents, spreadsheets, and other electronic documents.

E-mail permits instant communication and transmittal of up-to-date information, similar to the telephone. Unlike current telephone features, however, e-mail may create a record of the information that is being transmitted.

E-mail is only one part of the expanding world of electronic messages. The latter is any communication using an electronic system either within an organization or with others in the outside world. These messages may be in the form of e-mail, electronic document exchange (electronic fax), electronic data interchange (EDI), or multimedia communications such as voice mail and tele/video conferencing. For the purposes of this chapter, the terms e-mail and electronic messages are used interchangeably.

An electronic message is composed of three parts:

- *Content.* The information we wish to communicate.
- *Transmission data.* Information about the identities of sender and addressee, and the date and time the message was sent.
- *Receipt data.* Information about the date and time of receipt of

the message, as well as an (optional) acknowledgment of receipt or access by the addressee.

Preserving e-mail, therefore, involves more than just preserving the content. We also must have a plan for preserving transmission and receipt data as well as other contextual information. Without this we will not have a complete record.

The complexity of preserving e-mail was illustrated with a recent federal court case, *Armstrong v. Executive Office of the President.* This case involving the electronic mail in the Reagan White House was called the Profs Case after the name of the IBM e-mail system in use at the time.[1] One of the central issues was whether or not e-mail messages were records that needed to be preserved.

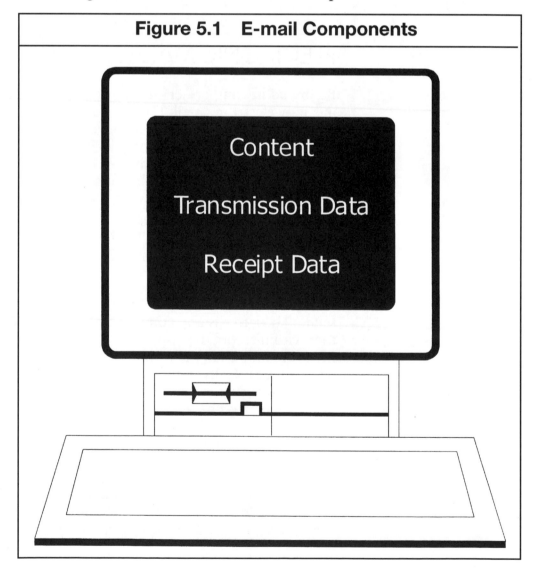

Figure 5.1 E-mail Components

Content

Transmission Data

Receipt Data

Once the court determined that e-mail could be a record, it went on to discuss some of the implications:

- E-mail was more than just a convenience copy that could be destroyed at will.
- An e-mail record involved more than content; it also contained context and structure that must be preserved in order to have an authentic record.
- Since e-mail was used for substantive business communications, it may have long-term value.

BASIC PRINCIPLES

Since the *Armstrong* case, archivists and preservation administrators have articulated a number of basic principles about e-mail.[2]

- *Electronic mail messages need to be handled as records.* Electronic mail messages transmitted through an organization's e-mail system may be records. The major task is determining when records need to be retained and when they should be discarded. This means determining which e-mail messages require long-term retention, determining who is responsible for making this determination, and establishing storage and disposition requirements for e-mail messages.
- *Electronic mail, in and of itself, is not a single record series.* The electronic mail system is a means of transmitting messages. E-mail is identical to regular postal mail that must be sorted. The e-mail system contains some important materials that will become records, some transitory items that can be quickly destroyed, some unwanted and unneeded junk mail, some personal mail for employees, and other types of mail that must be identified, sorted, analyzed, and acted upon appropriately.
- *There is no single retention period for all electronic mail messages.* Retention and disposition of e-mail messages depends on the function and content of the individual message. Thus, a universal rule that all electronic mail messages will be deleted after a defined period is not a comprehensive solution to managing e-mail. The various types of electronic mail require various retention periods—depending on whether they are of a long-term or more ephemeral nature.
- *The use of electronic mail is more important than the medium.* E-mail messages can be very informal, and yet provide an easy method for distributing information to others. The value and appropriate treatment for each electronic mail message is only determined when both the use and content of an individual message are clearly understood.

- *The end user manages electronic mail.* Electronic mail must be managed at the end user's desktop rather than from a central point. Each end user is responsible for managing records that are part of his or her e-mail system.

SYSTEM SELECTION AND IMPLEMENTATION

Organizations may be responsible for establishing the validity and accuracy of their e-mail systems in court; legal admissibility will largely depend upon the quality of the documentation available for the system in use and the care and preservation of the electronic records produced.

Documentation files are needed to:

- identify system hardware and software;
- formalize file naming conventions, back up, and security procedures;
- identify the sources and use of the information, as well as their confidential and nonconfidential status;
- outline quality control procedures and storage requirements;
- formalize employee training procedures;
- verify employee attendance at training sessions.

All features of e-mail systems, including messages, calendars, directories, distribution lists, and attachments such as word-processing documents need to be evaluated. For example, some electronic communication systems identify users by codes or abbreviated names and others identify the recipients of communication only by the name of a distribution list. With these systems, directories or distribution lists must be retained to ensure identification of the sender and addressee(s) of messages that are records.

ADMINISTRATIVE CONSIDERATIONS

The preservation of e-mail requires one to address a number of administrative considerations, some of them unique to e-mail and some of them common to other types of information. Here are some of these considerations:

- For convenient retrieval, e-mail needs to be filed systematically following standardized filing rules.
- Electronic mail files need to be indexed in an organized and consistent pattern, and reflect the way the files will be used and referenced. E-mail records maintained electronically have the potential advantage of supplying multiple access or index points.

- E-mail systems are designed to *communicate* rather than *organize and retain* messages. E-mail that needs to be preserved must be moved into a recordkeeping system, either paper or electronic. The recordkeeping system must preserve context and structure as well as content.
- E-mail messages fall into three broad categories: (1) transitory messages, including copies posted to several persons and casual and routine communications similar to telephone conversations; (2) records with a less than permanent retention period; and (3) records with a permanent retention period. An e-mail recordkeeping system must be able to separate messages into these three categories.
- Information systems managers routinely back up servers and the back-up media are recycled on a timetable. It is important not to rely exclusively upon this back-up for e-mail messages. If nontransitory e-mail messages are to be filed electronically, information systems managers need to be consulted. Appropriate storage locations need to be designated and users must be educated on classification and filing procedures so that the information will not be lost.
- Many computer systems have storage limitations, so that only 60 to 90 days of messages may be stored before operational problems are experienced. E-mail records that must be maintained in electronic format past that time should be downloaded to some other magnetic or optical storage medium. The retention period for the particular series is the best indicator of which storage medium to choose.
- Organizations that do not have the technical capability to maintain e-mail records for the full retention period in an electronic format should create an analog copy (paper or microfilm). Organizations with computers capable of maintaining e-mail records in an electronic format for the required retention may also decide that the organization is best served by printing e-mail records to paper or microfilm. In addition to the content, the following information needs to be retained for each message: name of sender; name of recipient; date and time of transmission, receipt, or both.
- All e-mail must be disposed of in a manner that ensures protection of any sensitive, proprietary, or confidential information. Magnetic recording media previously used for electronic records containing sensitive, proprietary, or confidential information should not be reused if the previously recorded information can be compromised in any way by reuse.

WEB PAGES

"In addition to digital documents which archivists must take a lead in managing, archivists must keep a close eye on digital information provisions, such as home pages on the World Wide Web and data warehousing projects on campuses. With the arrival of the Web, never before has so much information about offices, services, and information been available in such an accessible manner on college and university campuses and around the world."—William E. Brown, Jr. and Elizabeth Yakel, "Redefining the Role of College and University Archives in the Information Age."

It seems hard to believe that just a few short years ago there was no World Wide Web. It is impossible today to view a commercial or read a magazine without seeing a World Wide Web address or hearing about another "dot com." What are the preservation implications of this sea change? Over time, will we be able to access digital information on Web pages?

DEFINITIONS

As with e-mail, the beginning point must be clear definitions so we know just what we are trying to preserve. The World Wide Web Consortium provides the following definitions:[3]

- *Client.* "The role adopted by an application when it is retrieving and/or rendering resources or resource manifestations." The client accesses central data files and programs through a server.
- *Host page.* "A Web page identified by a URI containing an <authority> component but where the <path> component is either empty or simply consists of a single '/' only." Example: the Web page identified by *www.liu.edu* is a host page.
- *Link.* "A link expresses one or more (explicit or implicit) relationships between two or more resources."
- *Metadata.* "Machine understandable information for the Web." Metadata contains "information about information"—labeling, cataloging, and descriptive information structured in such a way that allows Web pages to be properly searched and processed, in particular by computer.
- *Uniform Resource Identifier (URI).* "A compact string of characters for identifying an abstract or physical resource." Also referred to as a Uniform Resource Locater (URL).
- *Web browser.* A program that enables the user to navigate the World Wide Web.
- *Web client.* "A client that is capable of accessing Web resources by issuing requests and rendering responses containing Web resource manifestations."
- *Web core.* "The collection of resources residing on the Internet that can be accessed using any implemented version of HTTP as part of the protocol stack (or its equivalent), either directly or via an intermediary."
- *Web page.* "A collection of information, consisting of one or more Web resources, intended to be rendered simultaneously, and identified by a single Uniform Resource Identifier (URI). More specifically, a Web page consists of a Web resource with

zero, one, or more embedded Web resources intended to be rendered as a single unit, and referred to by the URI of the one Web resource which is not embedded. Examples: An image file, an applet, and an HTML file identified and accessed through a single URI, and rendered simultaneously by the Web client."

- *Web resource.* "A resource, identified by a URI, that is a member of the Web Core."
- *Web site.* "A collection of interlinked Web pages, including a host page, residing at the same network location. 'Interlinked' is understood to mean that any of the Web site's constituent Web pages can be accessed by following a sequence of references beginning at the site's host page; spanning zero, one or more Web pages located at the same site; and ending at the Web page in question."
- *World Wide Web (WWW).* A communications protocol that allows multimedia access to the Internet.

WHAT SHOULD WE PRESERVE?

One of the biggest questions facing archivists and preservation administrators is: Which Web pages should we preserve? There already are millions of Web pages on the Internet with thousands more being added every day. Obviously, they don't all have long-term value—but how to select the valuable pages is far from obvious.

Archivists have a name for the process of determining value: appraisal. As archivists use the term, appraisal does not mean determining monetary value, though this may be one of several considerations. Rather, archivists use a number of terms basically meaning the same thing when referring to appraisal: historical value, long-term value, archival value, or research value.

The classic American statement of archival value, codified by Theodore R. Schellenberg of the U.S. National Archives, calls for preserving items with one or both of the following characteristics:

- *Evidential value.* The item documents the founding and substantive activities of the organization.
- *Informational value.* The item documents significant people, things, or events.[4]

One of the issues with informational value is how we define the word "significant." At one time, the "significant" people were the "great White fathers" like Washington and Jefferson. Recent scholarship has turned the definition of significance on its head, emphasizing the importance of documenting the average, ordinary, or everyday. As

"The need for effective, affordable, and sound measures to preserve digital information grows as organizations rely on electronic records for a significant portion of their corporate memory and as important aspects of our cultural heritage are stored in digital form."—*Electronic Records Research and Development: Final Report of the 1996 Conference Held at the University of Michigan.*

one would expect, this has dramatically expanded the category of informational value.

Archivists only now are beginning to apply these principles to the ever-expanding world of Web pages. While undoubtedly archival theory will continue to develop, the following are some general guidelines for determining the long-term value of Web pages:

Evidential Value

- The first Web page of an organization or institution may have evidential value.
- A Web page that protects rights or interests may have evidential value. For example, a company that manufactures a potentially dangerous consumer product, like a chain saw, may need to preserve the Web pages that contain warnings and disclaimers.
- A Web page might be preserved because it documents how a corporation moved into e-commerce, the selling of goods on the Internet. This page may be useful in the future in evaluating the success or failure of e-commerce initiatives.
- Some Web pages that are particularly good examples of the Web designer's art probably should be retained for their evidential value.

Informational Value

"One of the greatest ironies of the information age is that, while the late twentieth century will undoubtedly record more data than have been recorded at any other time in history, it will also almost certainly lose more information than has been lost in any previous era." Alexander Stille, "Overload: There's Just No Way to Save All the Information of the Information Age," *The New Yorker,* March 8, 1999.

- Does the Web page provide information of likely interest to people in the future? For example, a state geographical information system may document such things as pollution levels or toxic waste sites.
- A personal Web site of a politician or celebrity probably has informational value.
- Some Web pages have informational value because they are associated with the infamous. One example is the Web page of the Heaven's Gate Cult, which entered into a suicide pact in order to be lifted up by a spaceship hidden in the tail of a comet.
- A Web site that presents a company's entire product line may have informational value.

Compounding the situation is the fact that Web pages often are nothing more than a posting or publication of digital information that exists elsewhere. For example, a Web page that provides detailed campaign finance information may just be an access point to, or a duplicate copy of, a database that resides elsewhere.

Archivists and records managers use the concept of *record copy* to designate one copy of an item to keep for the full retention period. Applying this concept should enable us to determine whether the Web page or the underlying electronic record is the one we want to preserve. In many cases, the Web version will be the preservation copy because it already is in a format—Hypertext Markup Language, or HTML—that is a standard for which there is likely to be vendor support for the foreseeable future.

Figure 5.2   Web Page Accountability Exposure

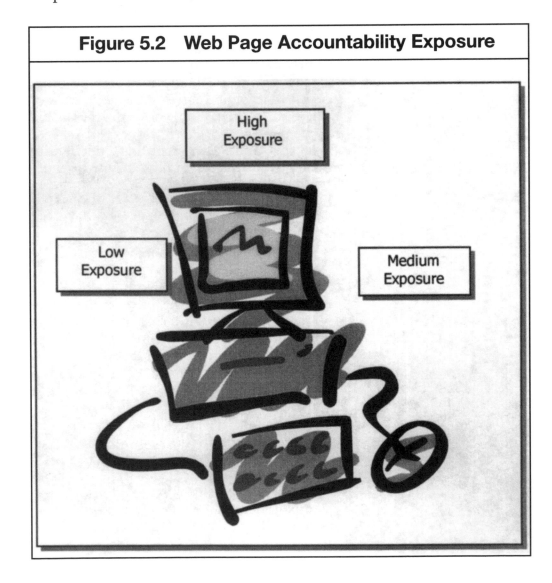

Accountability Exposure

Charles McClure and Timothy Spreh conducted research to develop records management and preservation strategies for electronic information contained in state and federal agency Web sites.[5] One of their key contributions was to define the *accountability exposure* of Web sites, which they call "the real likelihood of being called to account and the level of precision and detail the accounting will require." Accountability can take many forms: appearing before a legislative committee, answering a court's subpoena, and responding to calls from the public about what appeared on the Web site six months earlier. The private sector also will have other kinds of accountability, including meeting the needs of investors and other stakeholders. The key aspects of accountability are the ability to reconstruct what occurred in the past and the exactness of the reconstruction that circumstances may demand.[6]

McClure and Spreh identified three levels of accountability exposure: low, moderate, and high. A **low level** of accountability exposure is characterized by the following:

- Agency has a single Web site containing only copies of official agency publications.
- Agency controls who may post to the Web site.
- Experience shows that agency publications are not controversial.
- Publications have never been the subject of litigation and general counsel advises that little or no legal risk exists.
- Publications generate no unfavorable press reaction.
- Agency's public constituency appears satisfied with agency information services and urges electronic access via the Web site.
- Publications occasion little legislative interest.

Such Web sites have little accountability exposure. In these cases, the agency should keep basic Web site records such as documentation for the information system and standard operating procedures for its Web site. If the agency has satisfactory recordkeeping practices for its records not on the Web site, usually no additional measures are necessary.

A **moderate level** of accountability exposure occurs with Web sites with the following characteristics:

- Agency Web sites grow in number and complexity.
- Span-of-control problems grow; many offices now are posting to Web sites.
- Quality-control problems grow; e.g., several Web sites overlap in content but present conflicting information.

- Types of Web site use multiply; both purpose-prepared and interactive real time materials occur on Web sites.
- Original materials, not elsewhere captured in recordkeeping systems, sometimes appear on Web sites.
- Legal counsel is not consulted about potential legal liability of Web sites.
- Public affairs office advises that some materials could generate adverse public interest and prove controversial.
- There is substantial variability in management controls over whether Web site record-quality materials are transferred into recordkeeping systems.

If there is a moderate level of accountability exposure, the agency will need to take some additional measures to ensure the ability to reconstruct past Web site contents. In particular, McClure and Spreh recommend that an agency establish a historical log describing the contents of Web sites.

Some agency Web sites will have a **high level** of accountability exposure. These Web sites are characterized by the following conditions:

- Agency Web sites grow numerous and highly complex, with subsites and sub-subsites emerging.
- The contents of Web sites include ephemeral "bulletin board" postings, official agency publications, original materials not captured elsewhere in recordkeeping systems, official hearings, and other agency business created interactively in real time.
- Many different administrative arrangements arise for Web sites.
- The agency operates under intense public scrutiny; its publications, such as rulemaking, are controversial.
- Legal counsel advises that the Web site carries substantial liability for the agency. Litigation against the agency is frequent and acrimonious.
- Press coverage and usage of materials covered in Web sites is frequent; public interest groups watch the agency closely and often visit the Web sites.
- Legislative interest in the agency is active and vigilant.
- The public clamors for increasing electronic access to agency information holdings and expansion of Web site offerings. This makes the Web site practically essential to the agency's mission.

In these situations, there is a high likelihood that accountability issues will arise. In addition to the basic Web site records and the historical log mentioned above, the agency must take additional measures to ensure precise reconstruction of an exact copy of past Web site contents. One recommendation is that the agency maintain a comprehensive index of Web site contents over time. A second recommendation is that the agency take periodic "snapshots" of entire Web sites. If this is done electronically, the agency will be capable of reproducing the entire site contents exactly as they appeared.

To summarize, McClure and Spreh provide the following "primary records management principle" for state and federal agency Web sites:

> When materials are posted to an agency Web site **and** . . .
> the materials qualify as records, **and** . . .
> the materials have not already been adequately captured in an agency recordkeeping system, **then** . . .
> the agency must take steps to establish a linkage between the Web site and an agency recordkeeping system and transfer the records into the recordkeeping system.

With slight modification, this principle would apply to the Web sites of most organizations, both public and private sector.

PRESERVATION STRATEGIES

As with e-mail, Web pages are pushing the envelope of preservation strategies. The brave new world of hyperlinked network communication is forcing archivists and preservation administrators to develop new approaches. Some of the most fruitful of these approaches are:

- Selective downloads;
- Paper as "hedge";
- Virtual archives server;
- Snapshots of Web sites;
- Web page statistics;
- Business value of historical information.

Selective Downloads

One way that preservation administrators are beginning to address the preservation of Web pages is by doing selective downloads of information. The usual starting point is with information that we know has long-term value in its paper form. For example, if an archives has preserved press releases on paper, it may begin downloading the electronic versions that Public Relations now posts to its Web site.

Such downloads, however, can further confuse definitions and roles. In some state governments, there are specific legal definitions of "records" and "publications." The former are the responsibility of the state archives while the latter are the responsibility of the state library.

"From credit-card data to medical records, from airline databases to tax records, from electronic mail (e-mail) to digital film and sound, vast amounts of information about late-twentieth-century society exist in electronic form. This growing dependence of society upon digital information will change the fabric of the source material available to future historians. . . . Digital information is a cultural product, e-facts, and it forms an essential fragment of the cultural record of contemporary society."—Seamus Ross, "The Expanding World of Electronic Information and the Past's Future."

The problem is that a Web page is difficult to define: Is it a record, publication, neither, or both? A Web page may provide a list of campaign contributors (a record?) or take the place of a previously published annual report on activities (a publication?). Depending upon how we define the Web page, the responsibility for its preservation may fall upon two or more state agencies.

If one is considering downloading Web pages, I recommend starting small. This enables one to build up familiarity with the processes and identify problems while they still are manageable. It also enables one to move forward without a huge budget increase.

Paper as "Hedge"

During this time of transition, some archivists are printing out Web pages on paper to assure their preservation. These archivists are not willing to "bet the ranch" on a digital preservation copy.

Obviously, a paper copy has limitations:

- There is no ability to follow links, either internal and external
- Animations will be inanimate
- Dynamic Web pages will be captured as static.

Nevertheless, these archivists are viewing the paper as a copy of last resort: if all else fails and the promise of digital preservation is not realized, there still will be a paper copy in the files. Improvements to Electronic Document Management Systems (EDMS) may make the preservation of paper copies unnecessary.

Virtual Archives Server

If we decide that we are going to preserve digital copies of a Web page, especially in a pilot phase, one successful strategy has been to establish a "virtual archives server." This server can be a type of "archives play space" for the person becoming familiar with the transfer and preservation of digital files.

The archivist or preservation administrator either can locate and transfer pages manually, or develop scripts to do this automatically. Until the volume of pages becomes prohibitive, they can be kept "live" on the virtual archives server, perhaps even made available to others within the organization. As the volume increases, it may be necessary to off-load files to magnetic or optical media.[7]

Snapshots of Web Sites

There will be times when we want to preserve "snapshots" of all or part of a Web site. For example, we might determine that our preservation strategy is to make a copy of the organization's entire Web site every December 31. This would be a particularly appropriate strategy if we were motivated by evidential value.

Unlike paper copies, the digital snapshots would preserve hyperlinks, animations, and other interactive features. This would provide future researchers with the "look and feel" of today's Web sites.

There are a number of software packages designed to capture snapshots of Web sites. The software permits you to set the level of detail, including hyperlinks, that you wish to preserve.

Web-Site Statistics

It is now fairly common for Web sites to keep statistics on visits, also called "hits." Sometimes we see these statistics in the form of a "counter" at the bottom of the page; other times the statistical record keeping takes place in the background.

Web-page statistics can be a factor in appraisal decisions. For example, we might decide systematically to preserve the top five (or ten) Web pages within our organization. Or, we might be less formal and just use hits as one of many details to consider.

There is one word of caution in relying upon Web-page statistics. Some systems count each item on a page rather than just the page as a whole. For example, if there are ten images or graphics on a page, each image may be counted separately as the page is loaded, thereby inflating the count for that page.

If the archives or library establishes its own Web site, keeping hits may offer another way of demonstrating the value of its services. One archives in a major consumer products company is the most visited site in the entire corporation. This archives' site is particularly rich in photographs and other images.

Business Value of Historical Information

The World Wide Web is a two-way street. Not only are archivists and librarians trying to preserve its content, but they are using the Web's capabilities to promote historical awareness and understanding. As noted above, many archives emphasize their photographs and other images. In addition, historical timelines are a common feature on the Web sites of institutional archives. The more ambitious sites also include searchable databases and other interactive devices.

"Managing electronic records to ensure long-term availability is the most significant challenge facing the archival community." United States Congress, House Committee on Government Operations, *Taking a Byte out of History: The Archival Preservation of Federal Computer Records.* House Report 101-987. (Washington, DC: House of Representatives, 1990), 4.

CONCLUSION

At the beginning of this chapter, I likened preserving digital information to hitting a moving target. Not only must we care for existing fragile media and transitory formats, but the information industry keeps developing new hardware, software, and systems. E-mail and Web pages certainly will not be the last of these developments. What we learn from their preservation, however, may help us to focus on the next target and the one after that.

NOTES

1. For more on this case, see David Bearman, "The Implications of *Armstrong v. Executive Office of the President* for the Archival Management of Electronic Records," *American Archivist* 56:4 (Fall 1993), 674–689.
2. I am indebted to the Nebraska Secretary of State's Office, Records Management Division, for the opportunity to clarify my thinking on these points as part of a project to develop e-mail regulations for state agencies.
3. The definitions can be found on the Web site of the World Wide Web Consortium at *www.w3.org*.
4. For a summary of archival appraisal theory, see Gregory S. Hunter, *Developing and Maintaining Practical Archives: A How-To-Do-It Manual* (New York: Neal-Schuman, 1997).
5. The project was funded by the National Historical Publications and Records Commission (NHPRC). See Charles R. McClure and J. Timothy Spreh, *Analysis and Development of Model Quality Guidelines for Electronic Records Management on State and Federal Websites* at: *istweb.syr.edu/~mcclure/nhprc_title.html*. Page updated 1/98.
6. This information is taken from McClure and Spreh, *Analysis and Development of Model Quality Guidelines*, Chapter 6, "Guidelines for Electronic Records Management on State and Federal Agency Websites."
7. For disaster recovery reasons, all files should be backed up and placed in off-site storage. This applies to "live" files on the virtual archives server as well as files stored offline on magnetic or optical media.

6 DIGITAL IMAGING AND PRESERVATION

Unlike e-mail and Web pages, the topic of Chapter 5, digital imaging has been the subject of extensive research over the past decade. This research forms the basis for best practices in applying digital imaging to a preservation program.

This chapter shows the relationship between theory and practice in the following areas:

- What is digital imaging?
- Technical considerations in implementing an imaging system.
- Digital imaging and the preservation program.

WHAT IS DIGITAL IMAGING?

Before discussing digital imaging and the preservation program, it is important to define some terms. Cornell University, one of the leaders in applying digital imaging to preservation, defines digital images as "electronic photographs" scanned from original documents. "A digital image can accurately render the information, layout, and presentation of the original, including typefaces, annotations, and illustrations."[1]

CATEGORIES OF IMAGES

In general, the images that we seek to digitize fall into four categories. Each category of documents has certain characteristics or attributes that the preservation administrator needs to understand before beginning a document-imaging project.

- *Text or line art.* These documents are usually monochrome and have no tonal variation. Edges are distinct. Examples are texts, manuscripts, line drawings, woodcuts, typed or laser-printed documents, blueprints, maps, and music scores.
- *Continuous tone.* These documents feature smoothly varying gradations of tone and can be either monochrome or color. Examples include photographs and some art work.
- *Halftone or halftone-like.* These documents feature regularly spaced patterns of dots or lines, often placed at an angle. They can be either monochrome or color. Examples include line engravings and etchings.

- *Mixed.* These documents contain both text or line art and continuous tone or half-tone. They can be either monochrome or color. Examples include newspapers, magazines, and illustrated books.[2]

SCANNING TYPES

There are different ways to digitize these four types of documents. Selecting the proper scanning technique is one of the basic elements in a successful document-imaging program. Conversely, an inappropriate selection can doom the preservation administrator to frustration and the imaging program to failure.

There are three kinds of scanning techniques:

- *Bitonal.* Employs one bit per pixel (picture element) representing black or white. This is suitable for text, line art, and some halftone documents.
- *Grayscale.* Employs 2–8 bits per pixel to represent shades of gray. This is suitable for black and white continuous tone, halftone, and mixed documents, as well as some manuscripts.
- *Color.* Employs 8–24 bits per pixel representing color. This is suitable for all document types that contain color.[3]

As noted in Chapter 2, all of the above terms refer to "bit-mapped" or "raster" scanning. This is the process of scanning a document to obtain an image of it. In addition to raster scanning, there are two other types of scanning:

- *Optical Character Recognition (OCR),* which converts each number and letter in text to an ASCII code for data and word processing.
- *Vector Scanning,* which is used in Computer-Aided Design (CAD) systems to create engineering drawings.[4]

Unless noted otherwise, the rest of this chapter will deal with bit-mapped or raster scanning

Scanning of whatever type, however, is not an end in itself. Paul Conway has stressed that digital imaging technology is a *tool* and not necessarily a *solution.*

Acquiring an imaging system primarily to improve access to information now is almost as simple as choosing the right combination of available features to meet immediate management goals. Adopting the technology for preservation, on the other hand, requires a deep and long-standing institutional commitment, the full integration of the technology into our information management procedures

"Attitudes are changing rapidly. Liberals and conservatives alike—librarians, as well as publishers, scholars, and technologists—no longer view the electronic library in the manner of St. Augustine, who prayed, 'Lord, give me chastity—but not yet,' but as a concept whose time is upon us, not necessarily to replace the paper library, but to augment it in ways that combine the benefits of both." M. Stuart Lynn, "Digital Preservation and Access: Liberals and Conservatives."

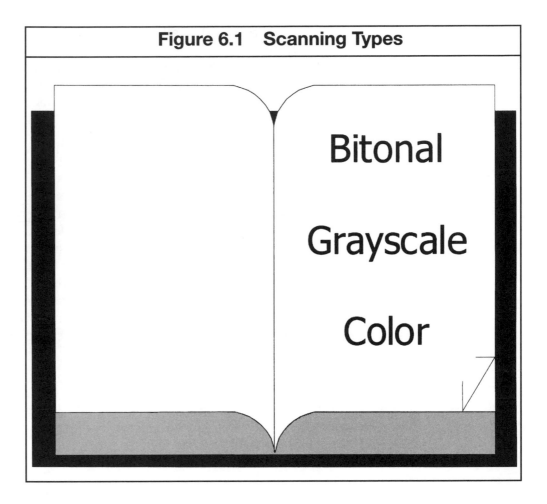

Figure 6.1   Scanning Types

Bitonal

Grayscale

Color

and processes, and significant leadership in developing appropriate definitions and standards of quality.[5]

ADVANTAGES AND DISADVANTAGES

Anne Kenney has noted that digital imaging technology has both advantages and disadvantages for the preservation administrator, especially when compared to microfilm. The major advantages are

- *Duplication without degradation.* There is no loss of quality as digital information is duplicated.
- *Ease of manipulation and enhancement.* The image can be optimized and transformed throughout its life cycle.
- *Preview capability.* After initial scanning, the image can be previewed before it is committed to storage.
- *Relative permanence.* Unlike paper, which deteriorates over time,

each time a digital image is transferred it literally becomes "as good as new."

- *Flexibility in output.* The output can vary depending upon user preferences or equipment constraints. In the future, there are likely to be additional output options for the digital images we create today.

Kenney also points out three major disadvantages of digital imaging systems:

- *Intensive maintenance.* As hardware and software change, the digital images will need to be transferred to new systems and media in order to remain accessible.
- *Ever-changing technology.* The supporting infrastructure for digital preservation will never remain static. The preservation administrator will always be riding the wave of new technology.
- *Long-term commitment of funds and resources.* Our institutions need to realize that digital preservation is not a quick fix or a one-shot deal. Rather, digital preservation is an ongoing, open-ended commitment to the future.[6]

Since digital imaging has its disadvantages, any project must be carefully planned and implemented. The beginning point is understanding the technology issues and choices.

TECHNICAL CONSIDERATIONS IN IMPLEMENTING AN IMAGING SYSTEM

There are a number of technical issues in implementing a digital imaging system. Try as we might, there is no way for the archivist or preservation administrator to install an imaging system without addressing the following:

- Underlying principles;
- Selection criteria;
- Image quality;
- The hybrid strategy.

UNDERLYING PRINCIPLES

The most successful digital imaging programs begin by determining what they are trying to achieve with the technology. Rather than immediately plunging into the digital domain, they step back to clarify their underlying principles, assumptions, beliefs, and biases.

Three institutions have developed underlying principles that can help any institution developing a digital imaging program: The Library of Congress, Cornell University, and the European Union.

Library of Congress

The Library of Congress (LC) developed a list of eleven "underlying principles" to guide its digital reformatting efforts. While some of the principles apply primarily to LC, the following eight principles are likely to be relevant to a variety of institutions:[7]

- Retain an analog version of digitally-reformatted items until you are confident that the digital data will be accessible for as long, or longer than, the analog version. The analog version may be the original or a paper or microfilm copy.
- Minimize handling of the originals to assure the best digital capture of an undamaged original, as well as the longevity of the original item (if it is to serve as the analog version).
- Ensure that the digital master file will allow a broad range of future use by employing standards and best practices.
- Capture the highest quality image technically possible and economically feasible.
- Archive a digital master file that is free of, or minimizes, changes introduced by the reformatting process.
- Ensure the completeness of all materials by using the standards employed for preservation microfilm.
- Employ tools (like checksums) that will ensure the integrity of master files through back-up and migration.
- Employ standards and best practices for structural, administrative, and descriptive metadata that will optimize interoperability with national and international digital library efforts and facilitate the life-cycle management of the digital objects.

The last bullet point introduces the term "life-cycle management" of digital data. LC prefers this term to digital preservation because the latter can have two meanings:

- The preservation of digital data
- The use of digital technology to preserve analog data.

LC intentionally uses life-cycle management to "refer specifically to the progressive technology and workflow requirements needed to ensure long-term sustainability of and accessibility to digital objects and

"As libraries build digital collections, they face the challenge of ensuring the persistence of materials that are stored on fragile media and recorded using hardware and software that rapidly become obsolete. Digital preservation refers to the various methods of keeping digital materials alive into the future. In this specific sense, digital preservation is a critical component of digital libraries, although the means of accomplishing it still need considerable development."—Donald J. Waters, "Digital Preservation?"

to metadata."[8] Such precision in the definition of terms can avoid misunderstandings later in the preservation program.

Cornell University

A second institution that has tried to state its fundamental principles is Cornell University. Through several grant-funded projects, the Department of Preservation and Conservation at Cornell has conducted some of the most valuable research on digital imaging in the preservation environment. Cornell lists five "prejudices that shape [their] perspective on the use of digital imaging in libraries and archives."

- *Know and love your documents.* The task of defining the value of digital surrogates involves determining how well they reflect the attributes of the original. To do this, we must know our documents very well.
- *Create one scan to serve multiple uses.* Capture images at the highest possible quality, but match the conversion process to the information content of the original. Long-term value should be defined by the *intellectual content* of digital images, not limited by technical decisions made at the time of conversion.
- *Benchmark before you begin.* Forecast your likely outcome before beginning the project. Identify formulas that can be used to benchmark various aspects of image quality and system performance.
- *Manage with the full digitization chain in mind.* Consider up front the reverberations of initial decisions throughout subsequent stages of the image life cycle: scanning, indexing, file management, networking, display, and printing.
- *Select for success.* Take a conservative approach when beginning digital imaging programs in order to develop capabilities modestly, incrementally, and systematically.[9]

European Union

The European Union has developed guidelines for its member nations about how to manage electronic information. While these guidelines cover more than preservation uses of digital imaging, they do contain a number of general principles useful for our purposes:

- All the items needed for the initial record must be transferred onto the same medium.
- Links between the record and the rest of the archives system must be preserved (e.g., other reference records).
- The quality of the original document (contrast, size of characters) must be good enough to ensure the best possible printout

"We should be concerned about who does archiving and how, because in the last few years we have experienced technical difficulties in accessing data that were stored electronically as recently as the 1970s." Linda Beebe and Barbara Meyers, "The Unsettled State of Archiving."

after conversion to a digital format.
- Before scanning documents, a sample should be tested.
- Even if scanning is subcontracted out, the organization having the work done should check the digitized documents for quality and completeness.
- Forms should be designed with their possible conversion to electronic form in mind (font size, position of fields).[10]

Taken together, the general principles prepared by the Library of Congress, Cornell University, and the European Union can keep an institution from losing its central focus as it turns to some of the more technical aspects of a document imaging program.

SELECTION CRITERIA

Digital imaging for preservation purposes is a commitment of resources for the indefinite future. As such, digital reformatting should only be used for items of unquestioned long-term value. It is important to try to clarify what we are seeking to digitize before beginning a reformatting program.

The Library of Congress (LC) has been one of the leaders in digital preservation. LC's Preservation Reformatting Division recently developed selection criteria for its use in imaging projects. LC identified six criteria, many of which will be applicable to other institutions as well:

- *Value.* Priority is given to high-value, at-risk materials of national interest. A digital reproduction has the added advantage of reducing handling of originals.
- *Condition.* Top candidates for digital reformatting are items that cannot be used because they are damaged, fragile, or are on unstable media.
- *Use.* Strong candidates are items with a high reference demand or high retrieval costs.
- *Characteristics of originals.* Originals with different characteristics (bound volumes, loose paper) and physical formats (photographs, negatives) are suitable for reformatting.
- *Acceptability of the resulting digital object.* The end result of the reformatting process must meet the overall requirements of the Preservation Division.
- *Access aids.* Guides, indices, and other finding aids also are candidates for reformatting.[11]

Cornell University suggests that an institution consider factors in five areas when choosing materials for digital conversion: digital collection development, physical attributes, preservation considerations,

"If a historian in the year 2090 wants to retrieve information about this culture, this moment in history, the books just won't have it all. We're used to preserving books, but whose responsibility is it to preserve all this digital material?" Paul LeClerc, President of the New York Public Library, quoted in "World Libraries Grapple With CD-ROM," Associated Press, June 8, 1999.

cost implications, and access. The five areas and their related factors are:

Digital collection development

- Informational value of individual documents
- Collective value of groups of documents
- Distributed sources and multiple formats
- Relevance to other online sources (both data and metadata)
- Thematic unity/critical mass
- Multi-institutional initiatives

Physical attributes

- Physical dimensions
- Level of detail
- Single leaf or bound
- Quality and condition of originals
- Use and condition of intermediates (e.g., duplicate 35mm slide)
- Reflective versus transparent media
- Production process used (machine printed, hand produced, half-tone composition)
- Relationships of media (inks, pencil, crayon, watercolor, etc.) to support (paper, color of paper)
- Number of documents
- Variety of document types and genres

Preservation considerations

- Level of informational content that can be captured (essence, detail, structure)
- Replacement/surrogate/reference use
- Fidelity versus legibility
- Quality benchmarks for reformatting (preservation microfilm or photocopy)
- Disposition of the originals

Cost implications

- Cost of image capture and indexing
- Volume of material to be converted
- Requisite technical infrastructure to support varied user needs
- Institutional capability and commitment (e.g., archiving)
- Cost effectiveness over time (e.g., space savings)

"In this new age of digital imaging and optical recording technologies, widescale access to documents is no longer the enemy of preservationists. Access and preservation strategies are no longer incompatible. Digital imaging technology is the first preservation technology that has the potential to increase and expand access to recorded knowledge rather than limit and restrict that access." Charles R. Hildreth, "Preserving What We Really Want to Access, the Message, Not the Medium."

Access

- Level of arrangement/documentation/indexing
- Frequency of use
- Uses to which material will be put (on-screen browsing, retrieval, reading, networking, printing, short term/long term)
- User requirements, perceptions, and technical capabilities
- Security considerations
- Legal restrictions

After making a careful selection of documents to digitize, the next step is to ensure we produce a quality image. All of our efforts are in vain if we do not capture an image faithful to the original and suitable for long-term preservation.

IMAGE QUALITY

As digital imaging has become a mainstream management technology, its purpose has changed. Gone from much of the commercial market is the *preservation* goal—maintaining the highest possible quality over time. In its place is the *access* goal of finding the minimum level of quality acceptable to the user. As Paul Conway emphasized, "We must reclaim image quality as the heart and soul of digital preservation." According to Conway, this has four aspects:

- *Equipment Calibration.* Equipment should receive regular maintenance as well as scheduled recalibration.
- *Resolution.* Image data should be captured at a high enough level to permit future manipulation. A minimum resolution is 300 dots per inch (dpi); 600 dpi or more may be necessary to maintain fidelity to the original.
- *Image Enhancement.* Images can be enhanced in several ways. Most common in a preservation environment is the "cleaning up" of images before they are stored. Since any enhancement may affect the integrity of the item and raise questions about authenticity, it should be done only according to previously approved policies and procedures.
- *Compression.* Compression techniques are used to reduce the volume of large files, especially images. Standard, nonproprietary compression techniques, such as the International Telecommunications Union's (ITU) Group 4 fax standards, offer the best hope of migrating images in the future.[12]

At the moment there are no standards for determining image quality for digital image capture. Different document types require differ-

"Though digitization is sometimes loosely referred to as preservation, it is clear that, so far, digital resources are at their best when facilitating access to information and weakest when assigned the traditional library responsibility of preservation. . . . Much is gained by digitizing, but permanence and authenticity, at this juncture of technological development, are not among those gains." Abby Smith, *Why Digitize?*

ent scanning processes. After much research and testing, Cornell University summarized the following guidelines (from the Cornell projects and others) for scanning various categories of materials:

- *Published text/line art.* 600 bpi bitonal is sufficient for replacement. This resolution level captures all significant information and avoids the labor and expense of item-by-item review.
- *Illustrated text.* 600 bpi bitonal scanning with enhancements is adequate for replacing most book illustrations where high contrast microfilm or photocopy is acceptable. Color illustrations will require 24-bit color scanning. Color oversize maps require 200 dpi, 24-bit color scanning.
- *Halftones.* Scan at 600 dpi bitonal (descreened) or grayscale at dpi equal to 1.5 times the screen ruling.[13] Color halftones will require 24-bit color scanning; begin at a resolution equal to 1.5 times the screen ruling.
- *Archival documents.* For typewritten, laser-printed, or most ballpoint documents, binary scanning at 300 dpi is adequate. Pencil, quill, or felt-tip pens require 300 dpi binary with gray. Damaged, stained, or faded documents require 300 dpi binary with gray or color. Papyri require 600 dpi, 24-bit color scanning.[14]

These guidelines will be useful throughout any preservation project, from initial planning to vendor selection and beyond.[15]

THE HYBRID STRATEGY

Because the advantages of analog and digital media tend to be complementary, many institutions are implementing a hybrid solution rather than an "either/or" approach. Basically, digital solutions improve access but come with the challenge of dealing with software and hardware changes over time. Analog solutions are stable and proven but are notoriously unfriendly to access. The hybrid strategy produces both microfilm masters and digital images to preserve and make accessible deteriorating research materials.

The research basis for the hybrid strategy comes from work conducted at Yale and Cornell Universities. Yale undertook a multiyear research project called "Operation Open Book," in which they digitized microfilm previously produced to preservation standards. This is called the "film-first approach." Cornell tested the other side of the equation: they digitized from original documents and produced computer output microfilm (COM) that meets preservation standards. This is called the "scan-first approach."[16]

The film-first approach has the principal advantage of meeting preservation objectives using well-defined standards for microfilm while permitting future digitization to meet access needs. There are other advantages as well.

- The photographic process has a very high resolution.
- When using existing film, some of the costs of preparation and capture were incurred before the imaging project.
- The equipment and service bureau elements are widely available.

However, there are also disadvantages to the film-first approach:

- There is a loss of image quality in the generations of analog film reproduction.
- Most microfilm is high-contrast film, which has a limited dynamic range for everything except text or line art.
- Some older microfilm is of poor or uneven quality.

The scan-first approach has the principal advantage of producing high-quality digital images directly from the originals, and producing microfilm from the images with little or no loss of quality. Some other advantages are:

- Image enhancement techniques can improve image capture.
- Intelligent scanning software can segment pages to optimize the capture of text and other elements (like photographs).
- The preview capability permits adjustments prior to conversion.

The following are the disadvantages of the scan-first approach:

- Digital resolution is lower than photographic resolution.
- Standards for preservation scanning are only now being developed.
- There are fewer high-resolution COM vendors than there are other types of service bureaus.[17]

Can't decide which to do first, scan or film? There is some high-end (and high-cost) equipment that will both scan and digitize on the same pass. For most institutions, however, purchasing this equipment will not be an option. These institutions will have to rely on their underlying principles and project goals to determine what to do first.

DIGITAL IMAGING AND THE PRESERVATION PROGRAM

As noted previously, digital-imaging technology is a *means* rather than an *end*. The end, or purpose, is to advance the preservation program. In order to know if digital imaging is advancing the preservation program, we first must develop goals for the program.

Lisa L. Macklin and Sarah L. Lockmiller have stressed the importance of setting goals before beginning an imaging project:

> An imaging project, like any other complex undertaking, should be designed to reach a clear set of goals. These goals should be clearly defined and articulated to all project participants and, often, to the ultimate user of the collection. . . . Goals should represent the fulfillment of needs for all stakeholders in the project, which include the end user or patron, administrators with oversight for the project, staff members involved in the project, granting agencies, etc. For archival collections, an important stakeholder is the researcher who will be using the collection many years in the future.[18]

In their opinion, a critical goal for any digitizing project should be the long-term viability of the image.

IN-HOUSE VS. OUTSOURCING

The archivist or preservation administrator considering a document imaging program will have an important practical question to answer: Who will actually do the work? The answer to this question will have a major impact on project scheduling and costs.

The "work" involves a number of steps that usually happen in the following sequence:

1. *Document preparation.* The removal of staples and other fasteners, and the flattening and cleaning of documents.
2. *Conversion.* The scanning of documents, with or without optical character recognition.
3. *Image enhancement.* The "cleaning up" of images or the bringing out of faint details.
4. *Intellectual control.* The naming, indexing, and encoding of images (metadata creation).
5. *Bibliographic control.* Entering information into catalogs or finding aids.
6. *Quality control.* Monitoring of work processes, inspection of images, and review of metadata.[19]

Each of these tasks can be performed in-house (using the institution's own staff) or outsourced (using a contractor). Ultimately, the choice must relate back to the institution's goals, as discussed in the previous section. In the words of Ann Kenney and Stephen Chapman:

There are major difficulties associated with outsourcing services when project goals are not clearly defined by the institution and communicated to the vendor. The responsibility for articulating requirements falls squarely on the institution itself. Before considering whether outsourcing is a viable alternative, an institution must have a good understanding of the near- and long-term goals of an imaging initiative, assess the collections to be converted and benchmark conversion requirements, define metadata requirements and users' needs, locate potential vendors, evaluate vendor claims and products, adopt policies and procedures for various functions, and define institutional and vendor responsibilities. As institutions develop a firm sense of their requirements and a confidence in what vendors can provide, outsourcing imaging services becomes a viable option.[20]

An **in-house approach** has a number of advantages:

- *Learning by doing.* The institution develops expertise as the project progresses.
- *Incremental definition of requirements.* The institution does not have to define all aspects of the project before beginning.
- *Maintenance of control.* The institution retains tight control over the full range of imaging operations.
- *Providing of security.* The institution can provide security and proper handling of fragile items.
- *Maintaining quality assurance.* The institution is responsible for quality control of all steps.
- *Cultivating relationships with manufacturers.* The institution can develop a relationship with the hardware and software vendors.

The in-house approach, however, does have a number of drawbacks. Among them are:

- *Required investment.* The institution must make a larger institutional investment to establish the infrastructure.
- *Limited production capabilities.* The institution cannot increase production to meet short-term requirements.
- *Limited staffing expertise.* Some technical aspects of the imaging process may be beyond the abilities of the institution's staff.
- *No set per-image costs.* The institution pays all costs of staff and equipment—which can vary from week to week—rather than paying a flat, per-image cost to a vendor.

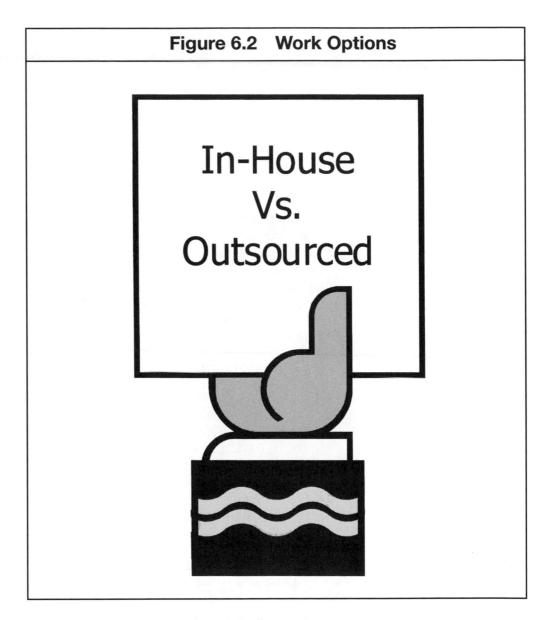

Figure 6.2   Work Options

In-House
Vs.
Outsourced

The **outsourcing approach** generally has advantages and disadvantages that are mirror images of the above. The advantages are: prices are set on a per-image basis; the vendor assumes the cost and risk of technological obsolescence; the vendor can be required to meet periods of high volume; and the vendor provides staff expertise across a range of functions. The disadvantages are: that the library/archives staff may not develop expertise; the institution is one step removed from the control of operations; the institution has to spend time communicating and negotiating with the vendor; and there is vulnerability because of vendor market changes.[21]

The good news is that institutions have used both approaches, in-house and outsourcing, to meet their digital preservation objectives. In both cases, the best practice has been the same: defining institutional goals and objectives in advance and using those goals to measure the success of the project.

CONCLUSION

According to Paul Conway, integrating imaging technologies into a preservation program requires four primary commitments. We need to:

- transfer valuable information across technology systems as these systems emerge;
- deemphasize storage media formats as the central focus of preservation concern;
- shift that concern to the fundamental challenge of specifying and then obtaining digital image quality;
- recognize the importance of maintaining structural, that is, contextual, as well as content indexes.

Because of these four commitments, Conway thinks that *reformatting* may not be the correct term. He suggests the term *transformatting* because digital imaging involves transforming the format of information sources, not simply providing a faithful reproduction of the images on a different medium.[22]

As Conway implies with his concept of transformatting, archivists and preservation administrators are blazing new intellectual and practical trails by preserving digital information. We need to make certain that the trails do not lead to dead ends or even worse—cliffs from which we can fall to a painful institutional death upon the rocks of failure.

Based upon all their experience at Cornell, Anne Kenney and Stephen Chapman offer the following caution and exhortation:

Digital imaging is not for the faint of heart, but the potential rewards are quite compelling. To realize those rewards will take a commitment of resources. It also requires a commitment not only to learn about the technology but also to adopt a new way of thinking about how we librarians and archivists go about the business of identifying, preserving and making available cultural resources in a rapidly changing world.[23]

The next chapter continues the discussion of institutional commitment by focusing on the preservation of information systems rather than just individual documents.

NOTES

1. Anne R. Kenney and Stephen Chapman, *Digital Imaging for Libraries and Archives* (Ithaca, NY: Department of Preservation and Conservation, Cornell University Library, 1996), 1. A definition from a business perspective reads: "Electronic Image Management (EIM) is an automated, computer-based configuration of equipment, software, and usually telecommunication facilities that store and manage machine-readable, computer-processable document images—and their associated coded index—for on-demand retrieval." Don M. Avedon, *Introduction to Electronic Imaging,* 3rd ed. (Silver Spring, MD: Association for Information and Image Management, 1995), 9.

2. Kenney and Chapman, *Digital Imaging for Libraries and Archives,* 4.

3. Kenney and Chapman, *Digital Imaging for Libraries and Archives,* 4, 20. This book provides the best summary of technical issues involved with digital imaging programs. In particular, various types of scanners are discussed on pages 50–59.

4. Avedon, *Introduction to Electronic Imaging,* 67.

5. Anne R. Kenney and Paul Conway, "From Analog to Digital, Extending the Preservation Tool Kit," in Nancy E. Elkington, ed. *Digital Imaging Technology for Preservation: Proceedings from an RLG Symposium Held March 17 and 18, 1994, Cornell University, Ithaca, New York* (Mountain View, CA: The Research Libraries Group, 1994), 13.

6. Kenney and Conway, "From Analog to Digital," 18–20. For a detailed discussion of imaging technology, see Don R. Williams, "Data Conversion: A Tutorial on Electronic Document Imaging," in the same volume, pages 59–79. For quality control, see Shari L. Weaver, "Quality Control," pages 81–97 in the same volume.

7. See Library of Congress, "Principles and Specifications for Preservation Digital Reformatting," available at *lcweb.loc.gov/preserv/ prd/presdig/presprinciple.html*. For another set of criteria, see Columbia University's "Selection Criteria for Digital Imaging Projects," at *www.columbia.edu/cu/libraries/digital/criteria.htm*. The Columbia criteria are particularly noteworthy for the way they define the "added value" of digital capture.

8. Library of Congress, "Life-Cycle Management of Digital Data," available at *lcweb.loc.gov/preserv/prd/presdig/preslifecycle.html.*

9. Kenney and Chapman, *Digital Imaging for Libraries and Archives*, iii–vi. For the digitization chain, see page 48. For a helpful overview of networking, one of the key elements of the digitization chain, see Don M. Avedon, *Telecommunications in Document Management* (Silver Spring, MD: Association for Information and Image Management, 1997).

10. *Guidelines on Best Practices for Using Electronic Information: How to Deal with Machine-Readable Data and Electronic Documents,* updated and enlarged edition (Luxembourg: Office for Official Publications of the European Communities, 1997), 24.

11. "Selection Criteria for Preservation Digital Reformatting," available at *lcweb.loc.gov/preserv/prd/presdig/presselection.html.*

12. Kenney and Conway, "From Analog to Digital," 16.

13. Cornell defines "screen ruling" as "the distance between dots placed at an angle." The formula for screen ruling is <u>screen ruling = 1/d</u>. See Kenney and Chapman, *Digital Imaging for Libraries and Archives*, 27.

14. Kenney and Chapman, *Digital Imaging for Libraries and Archives*, 33.

15. For a general discussion of quality control that is applicable to business document imaging solutions as well as preservation systems, see Don Avedon, *Quality Control of Electronic Images* (Silver Spring, MD: Association for Information and Image Management, 1997).

16. For more on these projects, see: Paul Conway and Shari Weaver, *The Setup Phase of Project Open Book: A Report to the Commission on Preservation and Access on the Status of an Effort to Convert Microfilm to Digital Imagery* (Washington, DC: Commission on Preservation and Access, 1994). Paul Conway, "Selecting Microfilm for Digital Preservation: A Case Study from Project Open Book," *Library Resources and Technical Services*, 40:1 (January 1996), 67–77. Anne R. Kenney and Lynn K. Personius, *A Testbed for Advancing the Role of Digital Technologies for Library Preservation and Access: Final Report by Cornell University to the Commission on Preservation and Access* (Washington, DC: Commission on Preservation and Access, 1993). Anne R. Kenney, "Digital-to-Microfilm Conversion: An Interim Preservation Solution," *Library Resources and Technical Services* (October 1993), 380-402; (January 1994), 87–95.

17. Kenney and Chapman, *Digital Imaging for Libraries and Archives*, 181–184.

18. Lisa L. Macklin and Sarah L. Lockmiller, *Digital Imaging of Pho-*

tographs: A Practical Approach to Workflow Design and Project Management (Chicago: American Library Association, 1999), 1.

19. Kenney and Chapman, *Digital Imaging for Libraries and Archives*, 142. Librarians have long known the value of indexing. The business community, however, is only now coming to a realization of its importance, largely because of the challenge posed by electronic documents. See Susan L. Cisco and Tom Dale, *Indexing Business Records: The Value Proposition* (Silver Spring, MD: Association for Information and Image Management, 1998).

20. Kenney and Chapman, *Digital Imaging for Libraries and Archives*, 141.

21. Kenney and Chapman, *Digital Imaging for Libraries and Archives*, 140–141.

22. Kenney and Conway, "From Analog to Digital," 17.

23. Kenney and Chapman, *Digital Imaging for Libraries and Archives*, vi.

7 PRESERVING THE INFORMATION SYSTEM

While preserving physical media and file formats is important and necessary, this alone will not be sufficient for preserving digital information in many institutional settings. As noted previously, preservation in a digital environment involves the *system* as well as the *information*. Both aspects must be addressed in a preservation program.

One concern immediately comes to mind: preserving an information system or information environment over time is likely to be an expensive proposition. Will my library or archives have sufficient resources to accomplish this task? If this undertaking is too massive, maybe we should not try to do anything and hope that the problem goes away. With such an approach the problem, indeed, will "go away"—in the form of unreadable information in antiquated formats on quaint media.

This chapter presents a methodology for moving forward with the preservation of digital information despite limited resources. The main point is that it is better to do something, even on a small scale, than to let the problem continue to grow unchecked. This chapter has three sections:

- Five assumptions about archival and preservation programs;
- Ten areas where the organization needs to make strategic decisions; and
- A seven-step approach to implementing the strategic decisions.

FIVE ASSUMPTIONS ABOUT ARCHIVAL AND PRESERVATION PROGRAMS

Implementing a digital preservation program will require financial and other resources. In requesting these resources, however, it is important to be realistic about what the institution is likely to provide. We also must be realistic about how others in the institution are likely to react to the new program.

I have phrased this realistic view in the form of five assumptions. While I think the assumptions will be valid for institutions of all sizes, they will be particularly relevant for small and moderately-sized institutions.

These are the five assumptions:

1. Digital preservation will never be the top priority.
2. We will never have sufficient resources to do things the ideal way.
3. If employees did a poor job managing paper, we should expect the same with electronic records.
4. Long-term plans won't sell.
5. We will not have the cutting-edge information technology available in other organizations or elsewhere in our own organization.

ASSUMPTION 1: DIGITAL PRESERVATION WILL NEVER BE THE TOP PRIORITY

"Only a fraction of libraries have full-fledged plans for archiving digital material. And while businesses increase the amount of digital information, libraries—and frazzled librarians—are left trying to figure out how to handle it all." Associated Press, "World Libraries Grapple With CD-ROM," June 8, 1999.

For most organizations, digital preservation will never be the top priority. This is so for a number of reasons:

- In most organizations, *preservation of any kind* is not a top priority. The focus often is on the present and the future with little concern for the past.
- Since a digital preservation program is likely to have significant start-up costs, it will be a "tough sell" to a management that does not already support a more general preservation program.
- Where digital information initiatives already are under way, they are likely to be focused on current rather than future needs. For example, staff working on a new information system for the manufacturing department are unlikely to think of long-term needs without some education by the preservation department.
- The Information Systems (IS) or Information Technology (IT) professionals, who control the computing and telecommunications infrastructures, are unlikely to be familiar with preservation concerns. For them, "archiving" means transferring a file to a tape or disk for off-line storage—usually for a brief period of time.
- Even in "preservation organizations," like national and state archives, the amount spent on digital preservation, though growing, is not likely to become the main expenditure of funds any time in the near future.

In brief, the preservation tail is not likely to wag the information dog in most organizations, especially until the value of a digital preservation program has been established.

ASSUMPTION 2: WE WILL NEVER HAVE SUFFICIENT RESOURCES TO DO THINGS THE IDEAL WAY

Textbook approaches or those developed in academic research environments will need to be modified in the real world to address resource realities. While most preservation work is a balancing act between needs and resources, this is even more the case in a digital environment.

A subsequent section of this chapter will deal with whether or not the preservation department takes custody of the digital information. Should the department take custody, it will need the following:

- Temperature- and humidity-controlled space to store records
- Fire-warning and suppression systems;
- Hardware and software capable of reading all of the formats accepted into the department;
- Regular budget allocations to purchase hardware and software as these change;
- Staff to store, copy, and retrieve the physical media on which the data are stored.

Even if the preservation department opts not to take custody of the digital information, there still will be significant resource requirements in a number of areas:

- Staff to work with the originating departments on the identification of digital information of long-term value;
- Funds for compliance monitoring either by the preservation department or another entity within the organization, such as internal audit;
- Funds to pay a third party for the physical management of the media used for storage and preservation.

The ideal program would be fully funded to accomplish all of the above activities. There would be adequate resources to store and preserve the physical media as well as to hire sufficient staff to work with information creators throughout the organization. Preservation administrators would have the time to develop plans to meet organizational priorities and to train employees at all levels in the intricacies of the digital preservation program. And pigs would fly!

ASSUMPTION 3: IF EMPLOYEES DID A POOR JOB MANAGING PAPER, WE SHOULD EXPECT THE SAME WITH ELECTRONIC RECORDS

Employees will not suddenly have a conversion experience. If organizing and managing paper has been a problem, there is every reason

"Those who subscribe to the all-digital future madness tell us that, in some unexplained manner, all the recorded knowledge and information we have will be digitized and kept in a system of universally accessible electronic archives. To see this for what it is, one has only to contemplate the trillions of dollars that it would take to gather and digitize all those records; the billions of dollars that it would take to maintain and make accessible this electronic Tower of Babel; and the fragility, mutability, and vulnerability of electronic records."—Michael Gorman, "Dreams, Madness & Reality."

to believe that the problem also will extend to the digital environment. How many people feel they have their e-mail under control? How many times have we had to look through numerous floppy disks trying to find the file that suddenly has become indispensable? Have our backup procedures really been adequate to enable us to recover easily from a hard-disk failure? It's not that most employees want to lose control over digital files; it's just that information keeps arriving at a faster pace and in greater volume.

The reality of this digital overload, combined with habits of poor records management and preservation carried over from the paper environment, should give the archivist and preservation administrator pause. A preservation solution that relies primarily upon "right thinking" by the majority of employees will be doomed to failure, unless there are vehicles in place to encourage and monitor that right thinking (an extensive training program, regular compliance monitoring, etc.).

ASSUMPTION 4: LONG-TERM PLANS WON'T SELL

We have all experienced the rapid pace of technological change. It seems that as soon as we purchase a new personal computer, a major industry announcement makes the equipment "obsolete." Granted, some of this advertised obsolescence is designed to fuel the purchase of even newer computers. Even so, there is no denying that information technologies seem to change faster than other technologies with which we come into contact with on a regular basis.

Our organizations and institutions are experiencing the same thing but on a larger scale. It becomes increasingly difficult to develop long-range technology plans when technologies change so quickly. For example, the World Wide Web was only developed in 1992 and experienced explosive growth in the past couple of years. The move to a Web interface for all organizational computing activities is something that no technology plan from 1990 could have anticipated.

In addition to the rapid pace of technological change, our organizations also experience regular turnover of staff in the information systems area. At the 1998 National Conference on Managing Electronic Records, there was a plenary session featuring two chief information officers (CIO). Many organizations have appointed CIOs to plan for and manage the complex information environments necessary to achieve institutional objectives. One of the CIOs at the above conference stressed that CIOs, as well as lower-level staff members, turn over regularly, often in as little as 18 months. As he explained it, within this time poorly performing information professionals would be fired, while excellent performers would be lured away by other organizations.

The bottom line, according to this CIO, is that any plans for digital

"Directing a state archives at the end of the twentieth century is like trying to walk across nineteenth-century London in the fog. Odd shapes loom up suddenly, voices are muffled and often unintelligible, and pedestrians bump into you and disappear. . . . Technology is like a stray dog that has joined the archivist in the middle of this journey. Depending on how it's handled, the dog may either inflict a painful bite or, suddenly docile, lead one safely through the city." Roy Turnbaugh, "Information Technology, Records, and State Archives."

information must show progress in the short term. If the archivist or preservation administrator presents a plan that will take five years to implement, the plan is unlikely to have the support of the CIO. Even if the current CIO supports the plan, much of the implementation will be left to information professionals not yet hired. This means that the archivist or preservation administrator will have to spend time educating these new staff members about preservation concerns and issues.

ASSUMPTION 5: WE WILL NOT HAVE THE CUTTING-EDGE INFORMATION TECHNOLOGY AVAILABLE IN OTHER ORGANIZATIONS OR ELSEWHERE IN OUR OWN ORGANIZATION

How many archives have been struggling for years to secure such low tech solutions as adequate space and shelving? How many preservation administrators have had to work without adequate funding for all that needs to be done? In this environment, the preservation program is unlikely to be at the forefront of organizational priorities for new information technologies.

This means that any strategies that we develop for preserving digital information probably cannot rely on the future availability of cutting-edge software solutions that will make our obsolescence issues disappear automatically. Yes, some large organizations will have the financial resources and staff expertise to implement emerging solutions. For the rest of us, we will have to devise preservation strategies that reflect existing budget realities and the likelihood of only modest increases.

STRATEGIC DECISIONS

It is important to develop strategies before plunging headlong into a digital preservation program. Such strategic thinking enables an organization, particularly one with limited resources, to focus energy and resources on the most pressing problems and the most promising solutions. Strategic thinking also promotes a long-range view that may prevent having to undo a prior decision that looked appropriate in the short term but later appears to be short sighted.

I have developed a series of ten strategic decisions framed as dichotomies, or polar opposites. Naturally, most real-world situations will tend not to be so extreme; rather, the course of action will fall somewhere in between. Nevertheless, thinking of the broadest possible range of options is a useful vehicle for focusing a discussion.

The ten strategic decision dichotomies are:[1]

1. "Go it alone" vs. "Work cooperatively"
2. "Think small" vs. "Think big"
3. "System design" vs. "Legacy systems"
4. "Identify the valuable" vs. "Destroy the worthless"
5. "Evidential value" vs. "Informational value"
6. "Custodial archives" vs. "Noncustodial archives"
7. "Media preservation" vs. "Content preservation"
8. "Keep digital" vs. "Transfer to analog"
9. "Audit compliance" vs. "Don't audit"
10. "Employee education" vs. "Leave them alone"

DECISION 1: "GO IT ALONE" VS. "WORK COOPERATIVELY"

Issue: Will the archives or preservation department try to devise a program by itself or will it partner with other departments?

This usually is one of the easier decisions. Few archives or preservation departments will have the resources to establish a program on their own. At a minimum, the archives usually will need to partner with the information services or the information technology department, the professionals responsible for the computers in an organization.

The best strategy is to have information services (IS) appoint a liaison to work with the archivist or preservation administrator. Using a liaison means that there will be a person in IS who learns to understand the specific concerns of the archivist or preservation administrator and who can serve as an advocate within the IS department.

Beyond IS, other partnerships also make sense. For example, the legal department or legal counsel will be interested in minimizing the potential exposure of the organization. As shown by recent court cases, digital information, especially e-mail, can be damaging to an organization during litigation. The legal department is likely to be interested in any initiative that helps to identify electronic records and regularly to destroy electronic records of no continuing value. Other partners will vary depending upon the type of institution.

DECISION 2: "THINK SMALL" VS. "THINK BIG"

Issue: Will the archives or preservation department focus only on small, safe projects or will it work on larger projects that might benefit the entire organization?

This decision really involves timing. Eventually the archives will need to address the larger, institution-wide preservation issue. The question is at what point in the process this happens.

One approach would be to develop knowledge and skills by focusing on small projects that are not likely to attract institutional attention. In this way expectations are low and there is less pressure on the archives or preservation department. Lower visibility, however, also tends to be accompanied by lower levels of organizational resources.

The other approach is to work on larger, more visible projects. Such projects have the possibility of providing greater return for the organization. However, if the archivist or preservation administrator wishes to address larger projects with more substantial issues, it is best to do so through pilot projects with one or more departments. Pilot projects enable the archivist to deal with big issues in an incremental way. Working cooperatively (decision 1) is essential for the successful completion of pilot projects. This is an approach I recommend highly.

DECISION 3: "SYSTEM DESIGN" VS. "LEGACY SYSTEMS"

> Issue: Will the archivist or preservation administrator spend time influencing the design of new information systems or will he or she focus on trying to salvage information from the numerous legacy systems still in use or already in storage?

Most archival research in the past three to four years has dealt with the "front end" of electronic records. Grants from the National Historical Publications and Records Commission (NHPRC) have led to the development of functional requirements for electronic records and the ongoing testing of those requirements.

The University of Pittsburgh received a grant to develop functional requirements and translate them into metadata specifications.[2] Subsequent testing has indicated that the cost of fully implementing the functional requirements may be beyond the means of many archives. For example, the city of Philadelphia had to scale down the number of functional requirements recommended for incorporation into new information systems.[3]

The University of British Columbia (UBC) has developed another "front end" approach to electronic records that draws upon diplomatics, a European science of document analysis developed during the Middle Ages.[4] The U.S. Department of Defense (DoD), which is trying to establish electronic records standards for its far-flung enterprise, has adopted the UBC approach. The DoD has begun testing and certifying software packages that meet its requirements.[5]

Legacy systems are a very messy problem—they fall far short of the "ideal" electronic records system. Working archivists and preservation administrators, however, cannot turn their backs on legacy systems as might academic researchers. The fear of a "black hole" of lost digital information stems from the knowledge that archival information is embedded in 30 years' worth of legacy systems.

Most archives will not have the luxury of experimenting with the development of functional requirements. Therefore I recommend that front-end strategies for electronic records focus on the following:

- Working with the information systems department to influence policy direction for new systems.[6]
- Advocating the use of *de facto* standards (ASCII for text, TIFF for images, etc.) rather than archival standards without broad industry support. Using *de facto* standards offers the best hope for future data migration.
- Waiting until the Department of Defense certifies specific software packages and then recommending the adoption of those packages within the organization. DoD's large market presence should guarantee ongoing vendor support for the software packages.

DECISION 4: "IDENTIFY THE VALUABLE" VS. "DESTROY THE WORTHLESS"

Issue: Will the archives try to select permanently valuable information or will it focus on destroying information of no long-term value?

At first glance, the difference between these two approaches may not be obvious. This mainly is a question of emphasis and how one tries to get to the body of information that ultimately will be preserved.

Selecting permanently valuable records involves the active identification of information. This identification only can take place if the archivist or preservation administrator works closely with people using the information now. This approach involves the archivist trying to find the needle in the haystack now rather than running the risk that the haystack becomes unintelligible because of hardware and software obsolescence.

The opposite approach, destroying information of no long-term value, is a Darwinian solution. This model results in the survival of the "fittest" information. The archivist or preservation administrator relies on the originator to determine which information continues to have value, primarily for current operations. The assumption is that originators will act responsibly, maintaining information for as long as needed. Once natural selection has taken place, the archivist or preservation administrator will make the final determination from the surviving records.

Many archivists are pessimistic about the efficacy of natural selection of digital information, even though it has long been part of appraisal theory, especially in the European tradition.[7] Skeptics doubt that individuals and organizations that have done poor jobs with paper-based records suddenly will "get religion" with digital information.

DECISION 5: "EVIDENTIAL VALUE" VS. "INFORMATIONAL VALUE"

Issue: In appraising electronic records for archival value, are both evidential and informational value given equal weight?

Traditional U.S. archival appraisal theory, as codified in the 1950s by T. R. Schellenberg at the National Archives, stated that archivists retain records that have either evidential or informational value (see Chapter 5):

- *Evidential value* means that the records document the founding and substantive activities of the organization.
- *Informational value* means that the records document significant people, things, or events.[8]

Much of the recent archival research has stressed electronic records as "evidence," particularly evidence of transactions. The U.S. National Archives, in fact, has adopted this language in some of its recent policy statements about electronic records. What has been missing from the discussion is an equal emphasis on informational value. This is especially important in the public sector where large numbers of patrons (like genealogists) primarily conduct research in records of informational value.

The decision about evidential or informational value also relates to the active versus passive selection discussed above. Creators of digital information may see a long-term need for evidence but are not likely to understand and appreciate the informational value sought by so many researchers. Allowing creators of digital information to decide what is preserved will skew the collection toward evidential rather than informational value.

"Who will decide what to save and how to save it, when it is becoming possible to pour terabytes of information into an unquenchable cyberspace of storage? When humankind's documentary record that is generated and distributed in digital format can be saved in virtually every textual version created, the dimensions of a selection process to identify that data worth preservation and that deserving discard reach incomprehensible limits."—Harold Billings, "The Information ARK."

DECISION 6: "CUSTODIAL ARCHIVES" VS. "NONCUSTODIAL ARCHIVES"

Issue: Should the archives or preservation department take custody of digital information or should it permit custody to remain in the hands of the records creators?

This is one of the most discussed dichotomies in the profession. Traditionally, archives have been custodial—they have taken physical possession and ownership of records. The other alternative is to permit the creators of electronic records to retain and manage them indefinitely.

David Bearman and Margaret Hedstrom are among the archivists advocating a switch to noncustodial electronic archives.[9] They emphasize a shift from "rowing" (the traditional practice of having the archives take custody and do all the work) to "steering" (where the archives sets policy and monitors compliance by the originating agencies).

In terms of electronic records, the U.S. National Archives long has taken a custodial approach. The Center for Electronic Records takes possession of electronic records and assumes responsibility for their preservation and access over time, including the costs of copying and migration.[10]

The Australian Archives illustrate the noncustodial option, which focuses on agency data management practices and assumes that the archives will not obtain custody except as a last resort.[11]

The main concern with the noncustodial approach is that originators traditionally have done poor jobs maintaining paper-based records over time. Inactive records often are "out of sight, out of mind" and relegated to space unsuitable for anything else. If this is how originators deal with records on paper, will they really commit the resources to long-term preservation of and access to electronic records?

DECISION 7: "MEDIA PRESERVATION" VS. "CONTENT PRESERVATION"

Issue: Will the archives or preservation department focus on preserving the physical media or will it focus on preserving the content of the electronic records?

A major portion of traditional preservation practice involves treating the record as artifact. With item-level conservation and restoration, the purpose is to preserve the medium as well as the message. Only with reformatting on microfilm or acid-free paper does the preservation administrator choose content over medium.

"For those growing tired of Y2K, here's another computer crisis to worry about: What if the data you so gallantly protected survive only to get trapped in digital oblivion in the not-too-distant future? That, experts warn, could be the unintended consequence of never-ending improvements in computer hardware and software. There is a risk that we won't be able to read older data, as the systems that support them become obsolete. Ask anyone who still has a stack of 8-inch floppy disks sitting around." Leslie J. Nicholson, "The Post-Y2K Bug."

With electronic records, content preservation is the only thing that makes sense. As noted previously, electronic media are fragile and transitory. At best, we can only preserve the medium for a few years before the data must be transferred to a new medium. The preservation of content clearly must be the focus of the electronic records archivist.

DECISION 8: "KEEP DIGITAL" VS. "TRANSFER TO ANALOG"

Issue: If electronic information has archival value, should the archives try to preserve it in digital form or transfer it to analog form for easier long-term preservation?

Another basic decision involves the long-term choice for medium: digital or analog. Both media have pros and cons.

- Using digital media maintains the maximum searchability and usability of the information. The disadvantage is that the data must be copied and converted on a regular basis.
- Using analog media simplifies the preservation problem because we can use a proven, stable medium like silver gelatin microfilm. The disadvantage is that there is a loss of functionality.

As noted earlier in this book, research libraries pioneering the use of digital imaging also are trying to strike a balance between digital and analog preservation options. Many are moving toward a hybrid solution where they scan for access but microfilm to preserve.[12] There is a justifiable concern over the long-term institutional commitment required for digital preservation.

The transfer of electronic records to analog form, especially Computer Output Microfilm (COM), is an option that archivists do not explore often enough. Because of the ongoing costs of and problems with digital preservation, COM is a technology that permits an institution to translate computer-readable records into analog records on microfilm, without first having to generate a paper copy. For example, files in an imaging system can be transferred to preservation-quality microfilm using COM. I think archivists need to expand the role of analog transfer in an electronic records program. This is an essential element in the preservation toolkit.

Archival reticence toward analog transfer parallels other archival mindsets. For example, until the National Archives defined the concept of "intrinsic value," there was little guidance about which original records needed to be retained after photocopying or microfilming. As a result, archivists tended to keep more than was really necessary.[13]

I believe archivists need to apply the concept of intrinsic value to electronic records. For how many records is the digital form *really* the only archivally acceptable form?

DECISION 9: "AUDIT COMPLIANCE" VS. "DON'T AUDIT"

Issue: If the archivist or preservation administrator gives originators more responsibility for electronic records, who will audit compliance, the archives or another department?

An archives cannot delegate *responsibility for* compliance: the archives will continue to be responsible for the long-term integrity of records. What an archives *can* delegate is the actual auditing *process*. Without an increase in resources, an archives is unlikely to be able to conduct time-consuming electronic records audits.

One strategy that makes sense is for the archivist or preservation administrator to try to partner with auditing entities within the organization. This also reinforces the fact that record keeping is a *line responsibility* rather than a *staff responsibility*: departments that create or receive records must manage them as part of general administrative responsibilities. Internal auditing, in turn, will monitor compliance with this requirement as it does with other management responsibilities.

DECISION 10: "EMPLOYEE EDUCATION" VS. "LEAVE THEM ALONE"

Issue: Will employee education be a central part of the program or not?

In an archives or preservation department with a small budget and limited staffing, it almost may seem as though spending time on employee education is a luxury. On the contrary, most archives will need an extensive education program in order to maximize their limited resources. Leaving staff alone is a short-term strategy that risks long-term failure of the digital preservation program.

This is not to say that an education program cannot take a phased approach. Indeed, it must. The first priority is to make the staff of the archives or preservation department aware of the specific requirements for digital preservation. From this foundation, the archivist or preservation administrator can build institutional knowledge of digital preservation through multiple media: workshops, presentations, articles in employee newsletters, and so on.

The key point is that training needs to be *systematic*, not piecemeal— as is most often the case. Part of this systematic effort might involve bringing electronic records issues into general staff orientation and training sessions. In particular, many organizations have found it helpful to use sessions on e-mail to talk about broader digital information concerns.

Addressing the above ten strategic decisions will help the archivist or preservation administrator to establish institutional priorities. The next step, implementing the priorities, is the subject of the following section.

SEVEN-STEP APPROACH TO IMPLEMENTING THE STRATEGIC DECISIONS

An organization needs a plan for implementing the strategic decisions discussed above. The plan, however, must take into account the assumptions detailed earlier in the chapter, especially the assumptions dealing with resources and equipment. What follows is a seven-step approach for the archives or preservation department dealing with a limited budget. The approach focuses on partnering with others in the organization in order to develop incremental solutions.

The Seven steps are:

- Understand the organizational context.
- Determine the role of the archives or preservation department.
- Define issues and concerns.
- Identify partners.
- Design pilot projects.
- Test approaches and solutions.
- Roll out the program to the entire organization.

STEP 1: UNDERSTAND THE ORGANIZATIONAL CONTEXT

Even though the archivist or preservation administrator may be a long-term employee of the organization, a digital-preservation program will require him or her to interact differently with other employees. The archivist or preservation administrator will have to become more involved with *active* records than is the case with most preservation programs. In addition, the archivist will need to have extensive dealings with information systems professionals, dealings that may not have taken place on the same scale previously.

As a first step, the archivist or preservation administrator will need to try to understand the organization *in its entirety*. This will involve reading annual reports and other documents that state the current con-

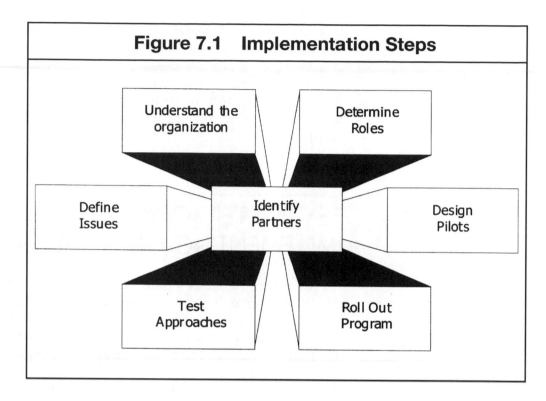

Figure 7.1   Implementation Steps

cerns of executives and administrators. The focus of the archivist must go beyond the care and feeding of inactive records on paper.

The archivist or preservation administrator also will need to schedule one or more meetings with the information technology (IT) staff. This can be intimidating for archivists who may not feel technologically comfortable and may fear that they do not know the secret handshake that provides entrance into the IT community. Nevertheless, the archivist or preservation administrator will need to understand, at least in broad brush strokes, the IT landscape and architecture. This is something that can deepen over time, perhaps as the archivist works closely with a liaison appointed by IT.

Also helpful at this point is to conduct one or more group meetings with electronic-records creators and users. There is perhaps no more efficient way to obtain an overview of the entire organization than holding such group sessions. If the archivist or preservation administrator provides coffee and danishes, there usually is a dramatic increase in attendance at the group sessions.

It is important to note that at this point the archivist or preservation administrator is not proposing solutions to the groups. Rather, he or she is looking to let people express themselves about the nature of their jobs and the ways in which they create and rely upon digital information. During subsequent steps the archivist or preservation administrator will again assemble groups to discuss potential approaches and solutions.

STEP 2: DETERMINE THE ROLE OF THE ARCHIVES OR PRESERVATION DEPARTMENT

Once the archivist has an overall sense of the organization, he or she should try to state clearly the vision of the archives or preservation department. From this vision will flow the role that the digital archives will place in the life of the organization.

Someone once referred to this as the archivist's "elevator chat." Pretend for a minute that you find yourself alone on the elevator with the president of your organization or chairperson of the board. As you stare up at the floor numbers gliding away ever so slowly, the president turns to you and says: "Tell me what the archives (or preservation program) does and why it makes a difference to the organization." What would you tell him or her in the minute or two that you had left? Would you have an elevator chat that would leave the president with a clear understanding of your department?

Clarity is even more important in the digital realm, where the technologies are both inspiring and intimidating. How will the archivist or preservation administrator justify his or her existence in this brave new world?

The possible roles are endless, limited mainly by resource requirements. However, these are some of the roles that other archivists and preservation administrators have established for their departments.

- *Advocate for historical concerns.* One obvious role is as an advocate for historical concerns. In many organizations, the archivist or preservation administrator may be the only person focusing on the past and future, rather than the present. This is especially the case in an information systems environment where the focus is on meeting the current needs of users without worrying about what will happen to the data in the long term.
- *Custodian of records.* As noted under strategic decisions, the archives or preservation department can take custody of all electronic records of long-term value. The alternate role is for the archives to opt to have custody remain in the originating department.
- *Internal consultant.* A third role for the archives or preservation administrator is as an internal consultant on digital preservation. In order to fulfill this role, the staff may need additional training in information technologies. The staff will need to "speak the language" in order to have credibility as an internal consultant.

"The experience of securing East German data files [in the West German Federal Archives after the collapse of East Germany and the reunification of the two countries] showed that the creating organizations are not the best custodians of their own machine-readable data. Many data files were no longer legible, and data documentation was at best incomplete, and in most cases missing. Federal offices cared for these electronic records only in so far as they could use them for their own purposes. This experience also showed that, in a world where state and society are in constant transition, it makes sense to have archivists engaged in electronic records management, and taking into their care records of long-term value." Michael Wettengel, "German Unification and Electronic Records," in Edward Higgs, ed., *History and Electronic Artefacts.*

"The growing use of electronic media has potentially profound effects on an organization's ability to retain, retrieve, and re-use its information resources. . . . In short, rapid changes in the use of electronic information media have outpaced institutional capabilities to manage them." T.K. Bikson and E.J. Frinking, *Preserving the Present: Toward Viable Electronic Records.*

- *Voice at the table.* A common role for the archivist or preservation administrator is to try to get a seat at the table where information issues are discussed. This involves getting appointed to committees or task forces dealing with the design and implementation of new information systems. While this will take time away from other duties, it is time well spent to assure digital preservation.
- *Information locator.* Many archives and preservation departments are opting for the role of "information locator." In this model, the archives becomes a one-stop-shopping source for informational resources whether maintained by the archives or the originating department. In the government sphere, this role is called a Government Information Locator System (GILS) and is found at both the federal and state levels.

There are other roles as well that the archives or preservation department can define for itself. Whatever role or roles the archives wishes to adopt, these must be communicated clearly to management and staff. A prepared elevator chat is of no use if it is not communicated to those outside of the archives or preservation department.

STEP 3: DEFINE ISSUES AND CONCERNS

The third step is to define the issues and concerns most relevant to the organization. This definition of issues will flow logically from the strategic decisions discussed above. For some organizations, the key issue will be the control of e-mail. For others, it will be the preservation of Web sites or the review of old computer tapes in inactive storage. It is important at this step, however, to present the issues in writing so that they remain the central focus of the organization throughout the rest of the preservation process.

Once the issues are defined, I recommend summarizing current research on the issues. This brief document should be presented in clear, straightforward language suitable for wide distribution throughout the organization—it should be free of technical jargon and acronyms. The purpose of the summary is to place the organization's efforts within the larger professional context and to stimulate additional thinking by management and staff.

As the archivist or preservation administrator develops this summary, he or she should ask questions that will be answered in the next two steps:

"Potentially, the information age offers the historian a Holy Grail of infinite memory and of instant, permanent access to virtually limitless amounts of information. But as the pace of technology change increases so does the speed at which each new generation of equipment supplants the last." Alexander Stille, "Overload: There's Just No Way to Save All the Information of the Information Age," *The New Yorker,* March 8, 1999.

- Which departments would make good partners to test solutions to the issues the organization identified as most important?
- What records would make good pilot projects to test approaches and solutions?

STEP 4: IDENTIFY PARTNERS

The next step involves "selling" the digital preservation program to potential partners within the organization. As noted above, most archivists or preservation administrators will not be able to go it alone. Therefore, any successful preservation program will have to flow from a partnership with others in the organization.

But how does one go about selecting partners? Start with these key steps:

- *Begin with your friends.* There is no point beginning with people who are resistant to the preservation initiative. Rather, it is better to begin with people who recognize the problem. At a later date, the program can be expanded to the entire organization, including the recalcitrant ones.
- *Try to address the concerns of the partners.* As tempting as it may be to try to focus exclusively on the concerns of the preservation department, this will not lead to a true partnership. The best way to build support within the organization is to listen to potential partners and give their concerns equal weight. Often during the course of discussion it will become clear how similar the interests of the preservation department and the partner department really are.
- *Try to find partners who can build positive word of mouth as the program progresses.* The ideal is to work with a partner who will enthusiastically tell others of your success. In this way, the "buzz" around the organization is positive rather than negative. Naturally, there only will be partner enthusiasm if we actually help partners solve their problems.
- *Be aware of organizational politics.* Sometimes the archivist or preservation administrator must consider politics when choosing partners. For example, it may be unwise to exclude another department head who also reports to your boss or to appear to be taking sides in existing organizational struggles.

The main point in selecting partners, however, is to focus on projects with the greatest chance of meeting objectives on time and under budget. All the other considerations mean nothing if we do not accomplish what we set out to accomplish.

STEP 5: DESIGN PILOT PROJECTS

The fifth step is to design one or more pilot projects in consultation with your partners. Each project should have the following components:

- *Objectives.* What do we hope to achieve in working with the partner?
- *Methodology.* How will we achieve the project objectives?
- *Time frame.* When will the project begin and end?
- *Responsibilities.* Who will accomplish the objectives? Which responsibilities belong to the archives and which belong to the partner department?

An example may help to clarify this step. Suppose that the public relations department has agreed to work with us on the transfer of quarterly reports now being created in electronic form. Table 7.1 gives possible answers to the above questions. A clear statement of project objectives and methodologies, similar to those in Table 7.1, will go a long way toward assuring the success of the pilot project.

STEP 6: TEST APPROACHES AND SOLUTIONS

The actual testing of approaches may take anywhere from a couple of days to several months. It is important to keep in mind that the partner is "lending" time and resources to the pilot project designed by the archivist or preservation administrator—this project probably will not be the partner's primary concern. This means that crises may arise that force the partner to slow down work on the pilot. The archivist or preservation administrator has to be ready for this. Usually adjusting the time frame for completion is enough to keep the partner involved in the project.

Remember that this is a pilot, or experiment. Therefore, it is common to have to adjust expectations and refine solutions as work progresses. While this may be frustrating, it is precisely the reason

Table 7.1: Designing a Pilot Electronic Records Program	
Objectives	To eliminate the transfer and preservation of paper copies of quarterly reports. To develop a seamless way of transferring digital copies.
Methodology	Since the quarterly reports are posted to the organizational Web site, we will transfer this electronic copy rather than the one created by word-processing software. This should cause the least interruption to departmental work processes.
Time Frame	The pilot project will begin on June 1. Within 30 days we will be ready to test the digital transfer. We anticipate needing one more month to iron out the kinks and finalize the plans for ongoing transfer.
Responsibilities	The archivist or preservation administrator will be responsible for securing space on a server where the files can be loaded. The Public Relations Department Webmaster will be responsible for writing a script to transfer the reports.

why we opted for an incremental solution rather than trying to implement a program throughout the entire organization at the same time. Better to learn from our mistakes on a small scale than to try to repair large-scale damage to our department's reputation.

Near the end of the pilot it should become obvious if we need to write policies or procedures before implementing the program on a broader scale. Once again, these policies and procedures are best drafted in consultation with the partners we already have cultivated.

Near the end of the pilot phase, it is helpful to prepare written summaries of the projects, focusing on lessons learned and experience gained. These written summaries will bring the pilot phase to closure by forcing the archivist or preservation administrator to reflect on project objectives and outcomes.

It is important to be honest in evaluating the pilot projects. Not everything will always go as planned and sometimes what seemed like a good idea before the pilot turns out not to have been so well conceived. As long as we learn from the experience, the pilot phase will have been well worth the time.

STEP 7: ROLL OUT THE PROGRAM TO THE ENTIRE ORGANIZATION

The final step involves implementing the digital preservation program throughout the organization. This requires four major activities:

> "From an archival perspective, which must address time-frames of 100 years or more, preservation of specific hardware and software may well be technologically and economically unfeasible." U.S. Congress, House Committee on Government Operations, *Taking a Byte out of History.*

- *Finalize policies and procedures.* If policies and procedures are in draft form, they need to be finalized before the program can be implemented broadly. Policies and procedures must be clear and consistent if the implementation is to be successful.
- *Prepare training and orientation materials.* The lessons learned during the pilot phase should be translated into training materials usable by all staff. This is the easiest way to institutionalize the program and to communicate its objectives to the entire staff. Training and orientation materials need to be appropriate for the organizational culture. In many cases, this will include both written instructions and presentations prepared using Microsoft PowerPoint or another presentation graphics program.
- *Conduct staff training seminars.* The easiest way to move from policy to program is by conducting training for all staff members. One approach is to train all members of a department at the same time. A second approach is to conduct training by staff levels (all department heads together, all secretaries together, etc.). As before, the decision on which way to proceed will depend on the culture of the organization.
- *Follow up with departments.* After the training sessions, it is important to schedule time for meetings with attendees. There

are bound to be questions about the nature and meaning of the program that the archivist or preservation administrator seeks to implement. The best way to deal with the uncertainties is by meeting face to face with staff members.

CONCLUSION

This chapter has stressed that it is better to do something with digital preservation, even on a small scale, than to let the problem continue to grow unchecked. To summarize, here are the key aspects of a practical approach:

- *Teamwork.* The archivist or preservation administrator cannot hope to "go it alone" with digital information. The problems are too massive and the solutions too expensive for an isolationist approach.
- *Standards and open systems.* The best way to minimize risk is by advocating open systems rather than proprietary solutions. These open systems are built around software and hardware standards.
- *Ongoing education at all levels.* From the beginning to the end of the project, it is important to take every opportunity to educate staff members at all levels about digital preservation. The educational component cannot be stressed enough.
- *Incremental solutions.* It is best to build organizational solutions from small successes, benefiting from lessons learned in the process. In this way the archivist or preservation administrator can maximize efforts and increase the odds of success.

Preserving digital information can be a daunting task. It is a task that someone must undertake, however, if our organizations are to retain their collective memories into the future. Never has the work of the archivist or preservation administrator been more important or more challenging.

I began this book with a millennial tale of digital preservation. The *New York Times,* in preparing a time capsule for the year 3000, thought that "a box full of stuff buried in a hole seems old-fashioned." The editors initially thought that a digital time capsule would solve their problems and provide the best window for our descendants to view our society and culture. As they learned more, the editors were surprised by the complexity of the digital preservation challenge and overwhelmed by its implications.

These feelings are quite common for anyone faced with preserving digital information. Analog media, though old fashioned, have the benefit of familiarity both in format and expected pattern of deterioration. These certainties are gone in the digital environment.

David Letterman's contribution to the time capsule, a "top ten list," stated that we were "on top of Y2K." Will our descendants also judge us to have been "on top of" preserving digital information? For good or ill, only time will tell.

NOTES

1. I developed these dichotomies over two years as a result of efforts to help archivists address the problems of electronic records. Consulting projects for the Florida Bureau of Archives and Records Management and the Ford Motor Company helped sharpen my thinking. In addition, in June 1998 I was fortunate enough to be asked to facilitate a meeting of 15 archivists from Fortune 500 corporations who wanted to share electronic records best practices. My thanks go to everyone involved.
2. For more information, see: University of Pittsburgh, *Functional Requirements for Evidence in Record Keeping*. Available at *www.lis.pitt.edu/~nhprc*. Page updated 1998.
3. Mark D. Giguere, "Automating Electronic Records Management in a Transactional Environment: The Philadelphia Story," *Bulletin of the American Society for Information Science* 23:5 (June/July 1997), 17–19. For a second project, see Phillip Bantin, "Developing a Strategy for Managing Electronic Records: The Findings of the Indiana University Electronic Records Project," *American Archivist* 61:2 (Fall 1998), 328–364. Also at Indiana University, *Indiana University Electronic Records Project, Phase I: 1995-1997*. Available at *www.indiana.edu/~libarche/index.html*. Page updated 1998.
4. For the UBC project, see *www.slais.ubc.ca/users/duranti/intro.htm*.
5. For more information, see *www.jite.fhu.disa.mil.recmgt/*
6. Some of the best work on building partnerships has been done at the State University of New York at Albany. For examples of their work, see State University of New York at Albany, Center for Technology in Government. *Practical Tools for Electronic Records Management and Preservation*. Available at *www.ctg.albany.edu/resources/abstract/mfa_toolkit.html*. Page updated June 29, 1999. Also *Models for Action: Practical Approaches to Electronic Records Management and Preservation*. Available at *www.ctg.albany.edu/resources/pdfrpwp/mfa.pdf*.

7. The classic statement of the European tradition comes from Sir Hilary Jenkinson of Great Britain. According to Jenkinson, the originator of the records, rather than the archivist, should make decisions about retention and destruction. In his words: "...for the Archivist to destroy a document because he thinks it useless is to import into the collection under his charge what we have been throughout most anxious to keep out of it, an element of his personal judgement [sic]; for the Historian to destroy because he thinks a document useless may be safer at the moment (since he presumably knows more history than the Archivist), but is even more destructive of the Archives' reputation for impartiality in the future: but for an Administrative body to destroy what it no longer needs is a matter entirely within its competence and an action which future ages (even though they may find reason to deplore it) cannot possibly criticize as illegitimate or as affecting the status of the remaining Archives." Hilary Jenkinson, *A Manual of Archive Administration* (London: Percy Lund, Humphries & Co., Ltd., 1966), 149.

8. T. R. Schellenberg, "Appraisal of Modern Public Records," in *A Modern Archives Reader: Basic Readings on Archival Theory and Practice*, eds. Maygene F. Daniels and Timothy Walch (Washington, DC: National Archives and Records Service, 1984), 57–70. The article was originally published in 1956.

9. See, for example, David Bearman and Margaret Hedstrom, "Re-inventing Archives for Electronic Records: Alternative Service Delivery Options," in *Electronic Records Management Program Strategies*, Hedstrom, ed. (Pittsburgh: Archives and Museum Informatics, 1993), 82–98 and David Bearman, "New Models for Management of Electronic Records," in *Electronic Evidence: Strategies for Managing Records in Contemporary Organizations*, Bearman, ed. (Pittsburgh: Archives and Museum Informatics, 1994), 278–289.

10. See National Archives and Records Administration, *www.nara. gov*. Page updated April 4, 2000.

11. See Australian Archives, *www.aa.gov.au*. Page updated March 30, 2000.

12. For example, see Abby Smith, *Why Digitize?* (Washington, DC: Council on Library and Information Resources, 1999). Available at: *www.clir.org/cpa/reports/pub80-smith/pub80.html*. Page updated February 1999.

13. National Archives and Records Service, "Intrinsic Value in Archival Materials," in Daniels and Walch, eds., *A Modern Archives Reader*, 91–99. The article originally was published in 1982.

SELECTED LIST
OF SOURCES

Multiple entries under a single author are arranged chronologically.

Abrahamffy, Steve, Kathryn Dan, Michael McCarthy, Greg O'Shea, Kerrie Scott, and Steve Stuckey. "Disposal in the Australian Archives: New Directions and New Challenges." *Archives and Manuscripts* 18:2 (November 1990), 203–212.

Ackerman, M. S., and R. T. Fielding. "Collection Maintenance in the Digital Library." *Proceedings of Digital Libraries '95*. Available at *csdl.tamu.edu/DL95/papers/ackerman/ackerman.html*. Page updated June 8, 1998.

Acland, Glenda. "Archivist: Keeper, Undertaker or Auditor." *Archives and Manuscripts* 19:1 (May 1991), 9–15.

Adams, Margaret O'Neill. "Punch Card Records: Precursors of Electronic Records." *American Archivist* 58:2 (Spring 1995), 182–201.

Advisory Committee for the Co-ordination of Information Systems (ACCIS). *Optical Storage: An Overview of the Technology and Its Use within the United Nations System*. New York: United Nations, 1993.

Allee, Verna. *The Knowledge Evolution: Expanding Organizational Knowledge*. Boston, MA: Butterworth Heineman, 1997.

Ampex Recording Media Corporation. *A Guide to Media and Formats*. Redwood City, CA: Ampex, 1990.

Applehaus, Wayne, Alden Globe, and Greg Laugero. *Managing Knowledge: A Practical Web-Based Approach*. Reading, MA: Addison Wesley Longman, 1999.

Archives Authority of New South Wales. *Documenting the Future*. Available at *www.records.nsw.gov.au*. Page updated March 28, 2000.

_____. *Managing the Message—Guidelines on Managing Electronic Records*. Available at *www.records.nsw.gov.au/publicsector/erk/managemsg/managemsg-01.htm*. Page updated February 23, 1999.

_____. *Desktop Management: Guidelines for Managing Electronic Documents and Directories*. Available at *www.records.nsw.gov.au/publicsector/erk/desktop/desktop-02.htm*. Page updated April 14, 1999.

_____. *Policy on Electronic Messages as Records*. Available at *www.records.nsw.gov.au/publicsector/erk/polem/messag.htm*. Page updated April 14, 1999.

_____. *Policy on Electronic Recordkeeping*. Available at *www.records.nsw.gov.au/publicsector/erk/polerk/erk-pol.htm*. Page updated April 14, 1999.

_____. *Corporate Memory in the Electronic Age: Statement of a Common Position on Electronic Recordkeeping.* Available at *www.records.nsw.gov.au.* Page updated March 28, 2000.

_____. *Records and Recordkeeping: Introduction.* Available at *www.records.nsw.gov.au/publicsector/rk/rrk/rrk.htm.* Page updated March 28, 1999.

Arms, Caroline (with Judith Klavans and Don Waters). *Enabling Access: A Report on a Workshop on Access Management,* Washington, DC: Digital Library Federation, 1999.

Arts and Humanities Data Service. *Strategic Framework for Creating and Preserving Digital Collections.* July 1998. Available at *ahds.ac.uk/manage/framework.htm.* Page updated July 14, 1998.

Association of Research Libraries. *Transforming Libraries: Issues and Innovations in Preserving Digital Information.* Washington, DC: Association of Research Libraries, 1997.

Atherton, Jay. "From Life Cycle to Continuum: Some Thoughts on the Records Management-Archives Relationship." *Archivaria* 21 (Winter 1985–1986), 43–51.

Atkinson, Ross. "Selection for Preservation: A Materialistic Approach." *Library Resources and Technical Services* 30 (October/December 1986), 341–353.

Australian Archives. *Keeping Electronic Records: Policy for Electronic Recordkeeping in the Commonwealth Government.* Available at *www.naa.gov.au/recordkeeping/er/keeping_er/intro.html.* Page updated March 30, 2000.

_____. *Managing Electronic Records: A Shared Responsibility.* Available at *www.naa.gov.au/recordkeeping/er/manage_er/intro.html.* Page updated March 30, 2000.

_____. *Managing Electronic Messages as Records.* Available at *www.naa.gov.au/recordkeeping/er/elec_messages/intro.html.* Page updated March 30, 2000.

Avedon, Don M. *Introduction to Electronic Imaging,* 3rd ed. Silver Spring, MD: Association for Information and Image Management, 1995.

_____. *Quality Control of Electronic Images.* Silver Spring, MD: Association for Information and Image Management, 1997.

_____. *Telecommunications in Document Management.* Silver Spring, MD: Association for Information and Image Management, 1997.

Awogbami, Papoola A. "Virtual Library: Cynosure." *New Library World* 97:1130 (1996), 32–33.

Bailey, Catherine. "Archival Theory and Electronic Records." *Archivaria* 29 (Winter 1989/90), 180–196.

Balas, Janet. "Building Virtual Libraries." *Computers in Libraries* 16:2 (February 1996), 48–50.

_____. "Preservation: A Special Concern." *Computers in Libraries* 17:6 (June 1997), 49–51.

Balon, Brett J., and H. Wayne Gardner. "Disaster Planning for Electronic Records." *Records Management Quarterly* 22:3 (July 1988), 20–24.

Balough, Ann. "The True Cost of Electronic Documents." *Records and Information Management Report* 14:1 (January 1998), 1–12.

_____. "Preserving Digital Information as a Record Copy." *Records and Information Management Report* 14:6 (June 1998), 1–16.

Banks, Paul N. *Preservation of Library Materials.* Chicago: Newberry Library, 1978.

_____. *A Selective Bibliography on the Conservation of Research Library Materials.* Chicago: Newberry Library, 1981.

Bantin, Phillip. "NHPRC Project at the University of Indiana." *Bulletin of the American Society for Information Science* 23:5 (June/July 1997), 24. See also *www.indiana.edu/~libarche/index.html.*

_____. "The Indiana University Electronic Records Management Project Revisited." *American Archivist* 62 (Spring 1998), 153–156.

_____. "Developing a Strategy for Managing Electronic Records: The Findings of the Indiana University Electronic Records Project 61:2 *American Archivist* (Fall 1998), 328–364.

_____. "Strategies for Managing Electronic Records: A New Archival Paradigm? An Affirmation of Our Archival Traditions?" *Archival Issues* 23:1 (1998), 17–34.

Barata, Kimberly J. "Functional Requirements for Evidence in Recordkeeping: Further Developments at the University of Pittsburgh." *Bulletin of the American Society for Information Science* 23:5 (June/July 1997), 14–16.

Bearman, David. *Archival Methods.* Archives and Museum Informatics Technical Report, 3:1. Pittsburgh: Archives and Museum Informatics, 1989.

_____. "An Indefensible Bastion: Archives as Repositories in the Electronic Age." In *Archival Management of Electronic Records*, edited by David Bearman. Pittsburgh, PA: Archives and Museum Informatics, 1991, 14–24.

_____. "Documenting Documentation." *Archivaria* 34 (Summer 1992), 33–49.

_____. "Diplomatics, Weberian Bureaucracy, and the Management of Electronic Records in Europe and America." *American Archivist* 55:1 (Winter 1992), 168–180.

_____. "The Implications of *Armstrong v. Executive Office of the President* for the Archival Management of Electronic Records." *American Archivist* 56:4 (Fall 1993), 674–689.

_____. "Managing Electronic Mail." *Archives and Manuscripts* 22:1 (May 1994), 28–50.

_____. "New Models for Management of Electronic Records." In *Electronic Evidence: Strategies for Managing Records in Contemporary Organizations*, edited by David Bearman. Pittsburgh: Archives and Museum Informatics, 1994, 278–289.

_____. "Archival Strategies." *American Archivist* 58:4 (Fall 1995), 380–413.

_____. "Item Level Control and Electronic Recordkeeping." *Archives and Museum Informatics, Cultural Heritage Informatics Quarterly* 10:3 (1996), 242–245.

_____. "Reality and Chimeras in the Preservation of Electronic Records." *D-Lib Magazine* (April 1999). Available at *www.dlib.org/dlib/april99/bearman/04bearman.html*. Page updated March 15, 1999.

Bearman, David, and Margaret Hedstrom. "Reinventing Archives for Electronic Records: Alternative Service Delivery Options." In *Electronic Records Management Program Strategies*, edited by Margaret Hedstrom. Pittsburgh: Archives and Museum Informatics, 1993, 82–98.

Beebe, Linda, and Barbara Meyers. "The Unsettled State of Archiving." *Journal of Electronic Publishing* 4:4 (June 1999). Available at *www.press.umich.edu/jep/04–04/beebe.html*. Page updated June 1999.

Bellardo, Lewis J. and Lynn Lady Bellardo. *A Glossary for Archivists, Manuscript Curators, and Records Managers*. Chicago: Society of American Archivists, 1992.

Bellinger, Meg. "Digital Imaging: Issues for Preservation and Access." In *Digital Image Access and Retrieval: Proceedings of the 1996 Clinic on Library Applications of Data Processing, March 24-26, 1996*, edited by P. Bryan Heidorn, and Beth Sandore. Urbana-Champaign, IL: University of Illinois, Department of Library and Information Science, 1997.

Bikson, T. K. "Organizational Trends and Electronic Media." *American Archivist* 57:1 (1994), 48–68.

Bikson, T. K., and E. J. Frinking. *Preserving the Present: Toward Viable Electronic Records*. The Hague: SDU Publishers, 1993.

Bikson, T. K., and S. A. Law. "Electronic Information Media and Records Management Methods: A Survey of Practices in United Nations Organizations." *Information Society* 9:2 (1993), 125–144.

Billings, Harold. "The Information ARK: Selection Issues in the Preservation Process." *Wilson Library Bulletin* 68:8 (April 1994), 34–37.

Blouin, Francis. "A Framework for a Consideration of Diplomatics in the Electronic Environment." *American Archivist* 59:4 (Fall 1996), 466–479.

Bolter, Jay David. "Text and Technology: Reading and Writing in the Electronic Age." *Library Resources and Technical Services* 31:1 (January-March 1987), 12–23.

Borgmann, Albert. *Holding On to Reality: The Nature of Information at the Turn of the Millennium.* Chicago: University of Chicago Press, 1999.

British Library. *Long Term Preservation of Electronic Materials: A JISC/British Library Workshop as part of the Electronic Libraries Programme, November 27–28 at the University of Warwick.* British Library R&D Report 6238. West Yorkshire, England: British Library Board 1996. Available at *ukoln.ac.uk/services/elib/papers/other/preservation.intro.html.* Page updated Nov. 24, 1998.

Brogan, Mark. "Regulation and the Market: A Micro-economic Analysis of Strategies for Electronic Archives Management." *Archives and Manuscripts* 22:2 (November 1994), 384–394.

Brown, Thomas Elton. "The Society of American Archivists Confronts the Computer." *American Archivist* 47:4 (Fall 1984), 366–382.

_____. "The Freedom of Information Act in the Information Age: The Electronic Challenge to the People's Right to Know." *American Archivist* 58:2 (Spring 1995), 202–211.

Brown, William E., Jr. and Elizabeth Yakel. "Redefining the Role of College and University Archives in the Information Age." *American Archivist* 59:3 (Summer 1996), 272–288.

Calmes, Alan. "To Archive and Preserve: A Media Primer." *Inform* 1:5 (May 1987), 14–17, 33.

Campbell-Kelly, Martin. "Information in the Business Enterprise." In *History and Electronic Artefacts*, edited by Edward Higgs. Oxford: Clarendon Press, Oxford University Press, 1998, 59–67.

Choo, Chung Wei. *The Knowing Organization.* New York: Oxford University Press, 1998.

Cisco, Susan L., and Tom Dale. *Indexing Business Records: The Value Proposition.* Silver Spring, MD: Association for Information and Image Management, 1998.

Cloyes, Kay. "The Journey from Vision to Reality of a Virtual Library." *Special Libraries*, 85:4 (Fall 1994), 253–257.

Cole, Timothy W. and Michelle M. Kazmer. "SGML as a Component of the Digital Library." *Library Hi Tech* 13:4 (1995), 75–90.

Coleman, James, and Don Willis. *SGML as a Framework for Digital Preservation and Access.* Washington, DC: Commission on Preservation and Access, 1997.

Columbia University. *Selection Criteria for Digital Imaging Projects.* New York: Columbia University, 1998. Available at *www.columbia.edu/cu/libraries/digital/criteria.htm.* Page updated June 6, 1998.

Commission on Preservation and Access. "Special Report: From Preservation to Access—Paradigm for the Future." *The Commission on Preservation and Access Annual Report*, July 1, 1992–June 30, 1993. Washington, DC: The Commission, 1993.

Conway, Paul. "Digitizing Preservation: Paper and Microfilm Go Electronic." *Library Journal* 119 (February 1, 1994), 42–45.

_____. *Preservation in the Digital World*. Washington, DC: Commission on Preservation and Access, 1996.

_____. "Selecting Microfilm for Digital Preservation: A Case Study from Project Open Book." *Library Resources and Technical Services* 40:1 (January 1996), 67–77.

Conway, Paul, and Shari Weaver. *The Setup Phase of Project Open Book: A Report to the Commission on Preservation and Access on the Status of an Effort to Convert Microfilm to Digital Imagery*. Washington, DC: Commission on Preservation and Access, 1994.

Cook, Michael. *Archives and the Computer*. 2nd ed. Boston: Butterworth, 1986.

_____. *Information Management and Archival Data*. London: Library Association Publishing, 1993.

Cook, Terry. "Appraisal in the Information Age: A Canadian Commentary." In *Archival Management of Electronic Records*, edited by David Bearman. Pittsburgh, PA: Archives and Museum Informatics, 1991, 50–56.

_____. "Easy to Byte, Harder to Chew: The Second Generation of Electronic Records Archives." *Archivaria* 33 (Winter 1991–92), 202–216.

_____. "Electronic Records, Paper Minds: The Revolution in Information Management and Archives in the Post-Custodial and Post-Modernist Era." *Archives and Manuscripts* 22:2 (November 1994), 300–328.

_____. "What Is Past Is Prologue: A History of Archival Ideas Since 1898, and the Future Paradigm Shift." *Archivaria* 43 (Spring 1997), 17–63.

Council on Library and Information Resources. *Collections, Content, and the Web*. Washington, DC: Council on Library and Information Resources, 2000.

Cox, Richard C. "The Record in the Information Age: A Progress Report on Reflection and Research." *Records and Retrieval Report* 12:1 (1996), 1–16.

_____. "Re-Defining Electronic Records Management." *Records Management Quarterly* 30:4 (October 1996), 8, 10–13.

_____. "Electronic Systems and Records Management in the Information Age: An Introduction." *Bulletin of the American Society for Information Science* 23:5 (June/July 1997), 7–9.

_____. "Why Records Are Important in the Information Age." *Records Management Quarterly* 32:1 (January 1998), 36–52.

_____. "Do We Understand Information in the Information Age?" *Records and Information Management Report* 14:3 (March 1998), 1–12.

Cox, Richard C., and Christopher Tomer. "Electronic Mail: Implications and Challenges for Records Managers and Archivists." *Records and Retrieval Report* 8:9 (November 1992).

Crawford, Walt. *Current Technologies in Libraries: An Informal Overview.* Boston, MA: G. K. Hall, 1988.

_____. "Moving toward Extended Libraries: Sensible Futures." *North Carolina Libraries*, 53:4 (Winter 1995), 162–171.

Cunha, George. "Current Trends in Preservation Research and Development." *American Archivist* 53:2 (Spring 1990), 192–202.

Cunha, George, and Dorothy Cunha. *Library and Archives Conservation: 1980's and Beyond.* 2 vols. Metuchen, NJ: Scarecrow, 1983.

Cunningham, Adrian. "The Archival Management of Personnel Records in Electronic Form: Some Suggestions." *Archives and Manuscripts* 22:1 (May 1994), 94–105.

_____. "Journey to the End of the Night: Custody and the Dawning of a New Era on the Archival Threshold." *Archives and Manuscripts* 24:2 (November 1996), 312–321.

Davenport, Thomas H., and Laurence Prusak. *Working Knowledge: How Organizations Manage What They Know.* Boston, MA: Harvard Business School Press, 1998.

Davidson, Jenni and Luisa Moscato. "Towards an Electronic Records Management Program: The University of Melbourne." *Archives and Manuscripts* 22:1 (May 1994), 124–135.

Dearstyne, Bruce W. "Knowledge Management: Concepts, Strategies, and Prospects." *Records and Information Management Report* 15:7 (September 1999), 1–14.

Delaware Public Archives. *Model Guidelines for Electronic Records.* Available at *www.archives.lib.de.us/recman/retention/elecrecpol.htm.* Page updated October 1, 1999.

Department of Defense, Joint Interoperability Test Command. *Design Criteria Standard for Electronic Records Management Software Applications.* Washington, DC: U.S. Department of Defense, 1997. Available at *jitc.fhu.disa.mil/recmgt/.* Page updated April 17, 2000.

DePew, John N. *A Library, Media, and Archival Preservation Handbook.* Santa Barbara, CA: ABC/Clio, 1991.

Dockery Associates. *Case Reference Repository.* Available at *www.finder.com/index.html.* Page updated March 5, 1998.

Dollar, Charles M. "Computers, the National Archives, and Researchers." *Prologue* 8:1 (1976), 29–34.

_____. "Appraising Machine-Readable Records." *American Archivist* 41:4 (October 1978), 423–430.

_____. *Electronic Records Management and Archives in International Organizations: A RAMP Study with Guidelines.* Paris: United Nations Education, Scientific and Cultural Organization (UNESCO), 1986.

_____. *Archival Theory and Information Technologies: The Impact of Information Technologies on Archival Principles and Methods.* Macerata, Italy: University of Macerata Press, 1992.

_____. "Archivists and Records Managers in the Information Age." *Archivaria* 36 (Autumn 1993), 37–51.

_____. *Authentic Electronic Records: Strategies for Long-Term Access.* Chicago: Cohasset Associates, 1999.

Dollar, Charles M., and Carolyn L. Geda, eds. "Archivists, Archives, and Computers: A Starting Point." *American Archivist* 42:2 (April 1979), 149–193.

Doorn, Peter. "Electronic Records and Historians in the Netherlands." In *History and Electronic Artefacts*, edited by Edward Higgs. Oxford: Clarendon Press, Oxford University Press, 1998, 304–316.

Drewes, Jeanne M., and Julie Page, eds. *Promoting Preservation Awareness in Libraries: A Sourcebook for Academic, Public, School, and Special Collections.* Westport, CT: Greenwood Press, 1997.

Dublin Core Metadata Initiative. "Dublin Core Metadata Element Set: Reference Description." Available at *purl.org/DC/documents/rec-dces-19990702.htm*. Page updated July 2, 1999.

Duff, Wendy M. "Ensuring the Preservation of Reliable Evidence: A Project Funded by the NHPRC." *Archivaria* 42 (Fall 1996), 28–45.

_____. "Compiling Warrant in Support of the Functional Requirements for Recordkeeping." *Bulletin of the American Society for Information Science* 23:5 (June/July 1997), 12–13.

_____. "Harnessing the Power of Warrant." *American Archivist* 61:1 (Spring 1998), 88–105.

Duffy, Jan. *Harvesting Experience: Reaping the Benefits of Knowledge.* Prairie Village, KS: Association of Records Managers and Administrators, 1999.

Duranti, Luciana. "Reliability and Authenticity: The Concepts and Their Implications." *Archivaria* 39 (Spring 1995), 5–10.

_____. "Archives as a Place." *Archives and Manuscripts* 24:2 (November 1996), 242–255.

Duranti, Luciana, and Heather MacNeil. "The Protection of the Integrity of Electronic Records: An Overview of the UBC-MAS Research Project." *Archivaria* 42 (Fall 1996), 46–67.

Du Rea, Mary V., and J. Michael Pemberton. "Electronic Mail and Electronic Data Interchange: Challenges to Records Management." *Records Management Quarterly* 28:4 (October 1994), 3–12, 59.

Durr, W. Theodore. "Some Thoughts and Designs about Archives and Automation, 1984." *American Archivist* 47:3 (Summer 1984), 271–289.

Eastwood, Terry. "Should Creating Agencies Keep Electronic Records Indefinitely?" *Archives and Manuscripts* 24:2 (November 1996), 268–285.

Electronic Records Research and Development: Final Report of the 1996 Conference Held at the University of Michigan, Ann Arbor, June 28–29, 1996. Ann Arbor, MI: University of Michigan, 1997. Available at *www.si.umich.edu/e-recs/Report/FRO.TOC.html.* Page updated 1997.

Ellis, Arthur, Imogen Garner, and Anna Rainford. "Network Document Access: Planning an Electronic Document Delivery Service; A Case Study." *Australian Library Review* 11:1 (1994), 67–74.

Ellis, Stephen. "Four Travellers, Two Ways, One Direction: Where to Now for Archival Practice." *Archives and Manuscripts* 24:2 (November 1996), 322–329.

Erlandsson, Alf. *Electronic Records Management: A Literature Review.* Paris, France: International Council on Archives, 1996.

European Union. *Guidelines on Best Practices for Using Electronic Information: How to Deal with Machine-Readable Data and Electronic Documents,* updated and enlarged ed. Luxembourg: Office for Official Publications of the European Communities, 1997. Available at *www.dlmforum.eu.org/documents/guidelines.html.* Page updated 1997.

Fletcher, Patricia. "Electronic Records Management in State Government: Planning for the Information Age." *Records Management Quarterly* 24:4 (October 1990), 26–32.

Florida Legislature, Joint Committee on Information Technology Resources. *Electronic Records Access: Problems and Issues.* Tallahassee, FL: Florida Legislature, 1994.

"Functional Requirements for Evidence in Recordkeeping." *Bulletin of the American Society for Information Science* 23:5 (June/July 1997), 10–11.

Gable, Julie. "Records Management for Electronic Documents." *Records Management Quarterly* 31:4 (October 1997), 15–19.

Gardner, Martin. "Secondary Use of Computerized Patient Records." In *History and Electronic Artefacts*, edited by Edward Higgs. Oxford: Clarendon Press, Oxford University Press, 1998, 120–137.

Garrett, John, and Donald Waters. *Preserving Digital Information: Report of the Task Force on Archiving Digital Information.* Washington, DC: Commission on Preservation and Access and Research Libraries Group, 1996. Available at *www.rlg.org/ArchTF/.* Page updated May 20, 1996.

Geda, Carolyn, Eric W. Austin, and Francis X. Blouin, Jr. *Archives and Machine-Readable Records*. Chicago: Society of American Archivists, 1980.

Geller, Sidney B. *Care and Handling of Computer Magnetic Storage Media*. Washington, DC: National Bureau of Standards, 1983.

General Accounting Office. *National Archives: Preserving Electronic Records in an Era of Rapidly Changing Technology*. Report to the Chairman, Committee on Governmental Affairs, U.S. Senate. Washington, DC: General Accounting Office, 1999.

Giguere, Mark D. "Automating Electronic Records Management in a Transactional Environment: The Philadelphia Story." *Bulletin of the American Society for Information Science* 23:5 (June/July 1997), 17–19.

Gildemeister, Glen A. "Automation, Reference, and the Small Repository, 1967–1997." *Midwestern Archivist* 13:1 (1988), 5–16.

Gilliland-Swetland, Anne J. "An Exploration of K-12 User Needs for Digital Primary Source Materials. *American Archivist* 61:1 (Spring 1998), 136–157.

_____. *Enduring Paradigm, New Opportunities: The Value of the Archival Perspective in the Digital Environment*. Washington, DC: Council on Library and Information Resources, 2000.

Gilliland-Swetland, Anne J., and Greg Kinney. "Uses of Electronic Communication to Document an Academic Community: A Research Report." *Archivaria* 38 (Autumn 1994), 79–95.

Ginsburg, Carol L. "The Realities of the Virtual Library." *Special Libraries* 85:4 (Fall 1994), 258–259.

Goerler, Raimund E. "Towards 2001: Electronic Workstations and the Future of Academic Archives." *Archival Issues* 17:1 (1992), 11–22.

Goldman, Patti A. "The Freedom of Information Act Needs No Amendment to Ensure Access to Electronic Records." *Government Information Quarterly* 7 (1990), 389–402.

Gorman, Michael. "Dreams, Madness & Reality." *Against the Grain* 8:1 (February 1996), 1, 16–18.

Grady, K., D. McRostie, and S. Papadopoulos. "Hunters and Gatherers: From Research Practice to Records Practice." *Archives and Manuscripts* 25:2 (November 1997), 242–265.

Graham, Peter S. "Long-Term Intellectual Preservation." In *Digital Imaging Technology for Preservation: Proceedings from an RLG Symposium Held March 17 and 18, 1994, Cornell University, Ithaca, New York*, edited by Nancy E. Elkington. Mountain View, CA: The Research Libraries Group, 1994, 41–58.

_____. *Intellectual Preservation: Electronic Preservation of the Third Kind*. Washington, DC: Commission on Preservation and Access, 1994.

_____. "Requirements for the Digital Research Library." *College and Research Libraries* 56:4 (July 1995), 331–339.

Granstrom, Claes, "Swedish Society and Electronic Data." In *History and Electronic Artefacts*, edited by Edward Higgs. Oxford: Clarendon Press, Oxford University Press, 1998, 317–330.

Green, Ann, JoAnn Dionne, and Martin Dennis. *Preserving the Whole: A Two-Track Approach to Rescuing Social Science Data and Metadata*. Washington, DC: Digital Library Federation, Council on Library and Information Resources, 1999.

Greenstein, Daniel. "Electronic Information Resources and Historians: A Consumer's View." In *History and Electronic Artefacts*, edited by Edward Higgs. Oxford: Clarendon Press, Oxford University Press, 1998, 68–84.

Greenstein, Shane. "Tape Story Tapestry: Historical Research with Inaccessible Digital Information Technologies." *Midwestern Archivist* 15:2 (1990), 77–85.

Grodsky, Jaimie A. "The Freedom of Information Act in the Electronic Age: The Statute Is Not User Friendly." *Jurimetrics* 31 (1990), 17–51.

Harrison, Donald F. "Computers, Electronic Data, and the Vietnam War." *Archivaria* 26 (Summer 1988), 18–32.

_____, ed. *Automation in Archives*. Washington, DC: Mid-Atlantic Regional Archives Conference, 1993.

Hazen, Dan, Jeffrey Horrell, and Jan Merrill-Oldham. *Selecting Research Collections for Digitization*. Washington, DC: Council on Library and Information Resources, 1998.

Hedstrom, Margaret. *Archives and Manuscripts: Machine-Readable Records*. Chicago: Society of American Archivists, 1984.

_____. "Understanding Electronic Incunabula: A Framework for Research on Electronic Records." *American Archivist* 54:3 (1991), 334–354.

_____. "Archives As Repositories: A Commentary." In *Archival Management of Electronic Records*, edited by David Bearman. Pittsburgh, PA: Archives and Museum Informatics, 1991, 25–30.

_____. "Electronic Records Program Strategies: An Assessment." In *Electronic Records Management Program Strategies*, edited by Margaret Hedstrom. Pittsburgh, PA: Archives and Museum Informatics, 1993.

_____. "Teaching Archivists about Electronic Records and Automated Techniques: A Needs Assessment." *American Archivist* 56 (Summer 1993), 424–433.

_____. "Descriptive Practices for Electronic Records: Deciding What Is Essential and Imagining What Is Possible." *Archivaria* 36 (Autumn 1993), 53–63.

_____. "Electronic Archives: Integrity and Access in the Network Environment." *American Archivist* 58:3 (Summer 1995), 312–325.

Hedstrom, Margaret, and Alan Kowlowitz. "Meeting the Challenge of Machine Readable Records: A State Archives Perspective." *Reference Studies Review* 16:1–2 (1988), 31–40.

Hedstrom, Margaret, and Sheon Montgomery. *Digital Preservation Needs and Requirements in RLG Member Institutions*. Mountain View, CA: Research Libraries Group, 1999.

Heminger, A. R., and S. B. Robertson. *Digital Rosetta Stone: A Conceptual Model for Maintaining Long-Term Access to Digital Documents*. Available at *www.ercim.org/publication/ws-proceedings/DELOS6/rosetta.pdf*.

Hendley, Tony. *The Archival Storage Potential of Microfilm, Magnetic Media, and Optical Data Disks*. Hertford, England: National Reprographic Centre for Documentation, 1983.

_____. *The Preservation of Digital Material*. London: The British Library Research and Development Department, 1996.

Hendriks, Klaus B. *The Preservation and Restoration of Photographic Materials in Archives and Libraries: A RAMP Study With Guidelines*. Paris: UNESCO, 1984.

Henry, Linda J. "Schellenberg in Cyberspace." *American Archivist* 61:2 (Fall 1998), 309–327.

Hickerson, Thomas H. *Archives and Manuscripts: An Introduction to Automated Access*. Chicago: Society of American Archivists, 1980.

Higgs, Edward. "Information Superhighways or Quiet Country Lanes: Accessing Electronic Archives in the United Kingdom." In *Playing for Keeps: The Proceedings of an Electronic Records Management Conference Hosted by the Australian Archives, Canberra, Australia, 8–10 November 1994*. Canberra: Australian Archives, 1994.

_____. "Historians, Archivists, and Electronic Record-Keeping in British Government." In *History and Electronic Artefacts*, edited by Edward Higgs. Oxford: Clarendon Press, Oxford University Press, 1998, 138–152.

_____. "The Role of Tomorrow's Electronic Archives." In *History and Electronic Artefacts*, edited by Edward Higgs. Oxford: Clarendon Press, Oxford University Press, 1998, 184–194.

Hildreth, Charles R. "Preserving What We Really Want to Access, the Message, Not the Medium: Challenges and Opportunities in the Digital Age." *Publications of the Essen University Library* 20 (1996), 78–95. Available at *phoenix.liu.edu/~hildreth/essen95.html*. Page updated 1995.

Hinneberg, Nancy B., and Amy W. Coughlin. "Electronic Information and the Records Manager." *Records Management Quarterly* 31:4 (October 1997), 20–26.

Hirtle, Peter. "Indexing Structures." In *Digital Imaging Technology for Preservation: Proceedings from an RLG Symposium Held March 17 and 18, 1994, Cornell University, Ithaca, New York*, edited by Nancy E. Elkington. Mountain View, CA: Research Libraries Group, 1994, 99–114.

Hofman, Hans. "Off the Beaten Track: The Archivist Exploring the Outback of Electronic Records." In *Playing for Keeps: The Proceedings of an Electronic Records Management Conference Hosted by the Australian Archives, Canberra, Australia, 8–10 November 1994*. Canberra: Australian Archives, 1994.

_____. "Towards a United but Distributed Archives of Europe?" In *History and Electronic Artefacts*, edited by Edward Higgs. Oxford: Clarendon Press, Oxford University Press, 1998, 331–338.

Horton, Forest Woody, Jr., and Kathleen Lannon. "Records Management and Information Management: Are They Having Fun Together Yet?" *Records Management Quarterly* 23:4 (October 1989), 12–18, 29.

Hunter, Gregory S. *Developing and Maintaining Practical Archives: A How-To-Do-It Manual*. New York: Neal-Schuman, 1997.

Hurley, Bernard, John Price-Wilkin, Merrilee Proffitt, and Howard Besser. *The Making of America II Testbed Project: A Digital Library Service Model*. Washington, DC: Council on Library and Information Resources, Digital Library Federation, 2000. Available at *www.clir.org/pubs/reports/pub87/contents.html*. Page updated December 1999.

Hurley, Chris, and Sue McKemmish. "First Write Your Disposal Schedule. . . ." *Archives and Manuscripts* 18:2 (November 1990), 192–201.

Hurt, Charlene. "Building the Foundations of Virginia's Virtual Library." *Information Technology and Libraries* (March 1995), 50–53.

Hyry, Tom, and Rachel Onuf. "The Personality of Electronic Records: The Impact of New Information Technology on Personal Papers." *Archival Issues* (1997), 37–44.

Indiana University. *Indiana University Electronic Records Project, Phase I: 1995–1997*. Available at *www.indiana.edu/~libarche/index.html*. Page updated 1998.

Ingwersen, Peter. "Information and Information Systems in Context." *Libri* 42:2 (1992), 99–135.

International Council on Archives, Committee on Electronic Records. *Guide for Managing Electronic Records from an Archival Perspective*. Paris, France: International Council on Archives, 1997.

_____. *Electronic Records Management: A Literature Review*. Available at *www.archives.ca/ica/english.html*.

InterPARES Project (International Research on Permanent Authentic Records in Electronic Systems). See *www.interpares.org*. Page updated February 3, 2000.

Jacobson, David C., R. Michael Lowenbaum, and John C. Koski. "Peril of the E-Mail Trail: Implementation of an Electronic Information Retention Plan Can Prevent a Disastrous Disclosure." *National Law Journal* (January 16, 1995), C1ff.

Jenkinson, Hilary. *A Manual of Archive Administration*. London: Percy Lund, Humphries & Co., 1966.

Jensen, Mary Brandt. "Copying for the Future: Electronic Preservation." *Document Delivery World* (June-August 1993), 29–31.

Jimenez, Mona, and Liss Platt, eds. *Magnetic Media Preservation Sourcebook*. New York: Media Alliance, 1998.

Jones, Norvell M. M., and Mary Lynn Ritzenthaler. "Implementing an Archival Preservation Program." In *Managing Archives and Archival Institutions*, edited by James Gregory Bradsher. Chicago: University of Chicago Press, 1989.

Jordahl, Gregory. "NARA Takes Steps to Protect the [Electronic] Historical Record." *Inform* 4:7 (July/August 1990), 10–11.

Kaplan, Hilary A., Maria Holden, and Kathy Ludwig, comps. "Archives Preservation Resource Review." *American Archivist* 54:4 (Fall 1991), 502–545.

Kathpalia, Y. P. *Conservation and Preservation of Archives*. Paris: UNESCO, 1973.

_____. *A Model Curriculum for the Training of Specialists in Document Preservation and Restoration: A RAMP Study With Guidelines*. Paris: UNESCO, 1984.

Katz, Richard N., and Victoria A. Davis. "The Impact of Automation on Our Corporate Memory." *Records Management Quarterly* 20:1 (January 1986), 10–14.

Keizer, Gregg. "Crumbling Infostructures." *Omni* 14:6 (March 1992), 56–61.

Kenney, Anne R. "Digital-to-Microfilm Conversion: An Interim Preservation Solution." *Library Resources and Technical Services* (October 1993), 380–402; (January 1994), 87–95.

_____. *Digital to Microform Conversion: A Demonstration Project, 1994–1996*. Ithaca, NY: Cornell University Library, Department of Preservation and Conservation, 1997. Available at *www.library.cornell.edu/preservation/com/comfin.html*. Page updated 1997.

Kenney, Anne R., and Stephen Chapman. *Digital Imaging for Libraries and Archives*. Ithaca, NY: Department of Preservation and Conservation, Cornell University Library, 1996.

_____. *Tutorial: Digital Resolution Requirements for Replacing Text-Based Material: Methods for Benchmarking Image Quality*. Washington, DC: Commission on Preservation and Access, 1995.

Kenney, Anne R., and Paul Conway. "From Analog to Digital, Extending the Preservation Tool Kit." In *Digital Imaging Technology for Preservation: Proceedings from an RLG Symposium Held March 17 and 18, 1994, Cornell University, Ithaca, New York*, edited by Nancy E. Elkington. Mountain View, CA: The Research Libraries Group, 1994, 11–24.

_____. "From Analog to Digital: Extending the Preservation Tool Kit." *Collections Management* 22:3/4 (1998), 65–79.

Kenney, Anne R., and Lynn K. Personius. *Joint Study in Digital Preservation. Report: Phase I (January 1990-December 1991). Digital Capture, Paper Facsimiles, and Network Access.* Washington, DC: Commission on Preservation and Access, 1992

_____. *A Testbed for Advancing the Role of Digital Technologies for Library Preservation and Access: Final Report by Cornell University to the Commission on Preservation and Access.* Washington, DC: Commission on Preservation and Access, 1993.

Kenney, Anne R., and Oya Y. Rieger. *Using Kodak Photo CD Technology for Preservation and Access: A Guide for Librarians, Archivists, and Curators.* Ithaca, NY: Cornell University Library, Department of Preservation and Conservation, 1998.

Kesner, Richard M. "Computers, Archival Administration, and the Challenges of the 1980s." *Georgia Archive,* 9:2 (Fall 1981), 1–18.

_____. "Microcomputer Archives and Records Management Systems: Guidelines for Future Development." *American Archivist* 45:3 (Summer 1982), 299–311.

_____. *Information Management, Machine-Readable Records, and Administration: An Annotated Bibliography.* Chicago: Society of American Archivists, 1983.

_____. *Automation for Archivists and Records Managers: Planning and Implementation Strategies.* Chicago: Society of American Archivists, 1984.

_____. "Automated Information Management: Is There a Role for the Archivist in the Office of the Future?" *Archivaria* 19 (Winter 1984–85).

_____. *Information Systems: A Strategic Approach to Planning and Implementation.* Chicago: American Library Association, 1988.

_____. "Group Work, 'Groupware,' and the Transformation of Information Resource Management." *American Archivist* 58:2 (Spring 1995), 154–169.

_____. "Information Resource Management in the Electronic Workplace: A Personal Perspective on 'Archives in the Information Society.'" *American Archivist* 61:1 (Spring 1998), 70–87.

Koulopouos, Thomas M., and Carl Frappaolo. *Electronic Document Management Systems: A Portable Consultant.* New York: McGraw-Hill, 1995.

Kowlowitz, Alan. "Appraising in a Vacuum: Electronic Records Appraisal Issues—A View From the Trenches." In *Archival Management of Electronic Records*, edited by David Bearman. Pittsburgh, PA: Archives and Museum Informatics, 1991, 31–37.

Kowlowitz, Alan, and Kristine Kelly. "Models for Action: Developing Practical Approaches to Electronic Records Management and Preservation." *Bulletin of the American Society for Information Science* 23:5 (June/July 1997), 20–24.

Kranch, Douglas A. "Beyond Migration: Preserving Electronic Documents with Digital Tablets." *Information Technologies and Libraries* 17 (September 1998), 138–148.

LaRue, James. "The Library of Tomorrow: A Virtual Certainty." *Computers in Libraries* 13:2 (1993), 14–17.

Laukner, Kurt F., and Mildred D. Lintner. *The Computer Continuum*. Indianapolis: Que Education and Training, Macmillan, 1999.

Leahy, Patrick. "The Electronic FOIA Amendments of 1996: Reforming the FOIA for On-line Access." *Administrative Law Review* 50:2 (1998), 339–344.

Lesk, Michael. *Image Formats for Preservation and Access*. Washington, DC: Commission on Preservation and Access, 1990.

_____. *Preservation of New Technology: A Report of the Technology Assessment Advisory Committee to the Commission on Preservation and Access*. Washington, DC: Commission on Preservation and Access, 1992.

_____. *Practical Digital Libraries: Books, Bytes & Bucks*. San Francisco, CA: Morgan Kaufmann, 1997.

Levy, David M., and Catherine C. Marshall. "Going Digital: A Look at Assumptions Underlying Digital Libraries." *Communications of the ACM* 38:4 (1995), 77–83.

Lewis, James D. "White House Electronic Mail and Federal Recordkeeping Law: Press 'D' to Delete History." *Michigan Law Review* 93:4 (February 1995), 794–849.

Library of Congress. *Challenges to Building an Effective Digital Library*. Available at *memory.loc.gov/ammem/dli2/html/cbedl.html*.

_____. *Selection Criteria for Preservation Digital Reformatting*. Available at *lcweb.loc.gov/preserv/prd/presdig/presselection.html*. Page updated December 12, 1999.

_____. *Life-Cycle Management of Digital Data*. Available at *lcweb.loc.gov/preserv/prd/presdig/preslifecycle.html*. Page updated December 29, 1999.

_____. *Principles and Specifications for Preservation Digital Reformatting*. Available at *lcweb.loc.gov/preserv/prd/presdig/ presprinciple. html*. Page updated January 4, 2000.

_____. *Phased Custody and Delivery of Digitally-Reformatted Resources*. Available at *lcweb.loc.gov/preserv/prd/presdig/presphase.html*. Page updated January 5, 2000.

Lievesley, Denise. "Increasing the Value of Data." In *History and Electronic Artefacts*, edited by Edward Higgs. Oxford: Clarendon Press, Oxford University Press, 1998, 253–264.

Loewen, Candace. "The Control of Electronic Records Having Archival Value." *Archivaria* 36 (Autumn 1993), 64–73.

Lowry, Charles B., and Barbara G. Richards. "Courting Discovery: Managing Transition to the Virtual Library." *Library Hi Tech* 12:4 (1994), 7–13.

Lowry, Charles B., and Denise A. Troll. "Carnegie Mellon University and University Microfilms International 'Virtual Library Project.'" *Serials Librarian* 28:1–2 (1996), 143–169.

Lyman, Peter. "What Is a Digital Library? Technology, Intellectual Property, and the Public Interest." *Daedalus* 125:4 (1996), 1–33.

Lyman, Peter, and Brewster Kahle. "Archiving Digital Cultural Artifacts: Organizing an Agenda for Action." *D-Lib Magazine* (July–August 1998). Available at *www.dlib.org/dlib/july98/07lyman.html*. Page updated 1998.

Lynch, Clifford. "The Integrity of Digital Information: Mechanics and Definitional Issues." *Journal of the American Society for Information Science* 45:10 (1994), 737–744.

_____. "Integrity Issues in Electronic Publishing." In *Scholarly Publishing: The Electronic Frontier*, edited by Robin P. Peek and Gregory B. Newby. Cambridge: MIT Press, 1996, 133–145.

Lynch, Clifford, and Edwin B. Brownrigg. "Library Applications of Electronic Imaging Technology." *Information Technology and Libraries* 5:2 (June 1986), 100–102.

Lynn, M. Stuart. "Digital Preservation and Access: Liberals and Conservatives." In *Digital Imaging Technology for Preservation: Proceedings from an RLG Symposium Held March 17 and 18, 1994, Cornell University, Ithaca, New York*, edited by Nancy E. Elkington. Mountain View, CA: Research Libraries Group, 1994, 1–10.

Lysakowski, Rich, and Zahava Leibowitz. *Titanic 2020: A Call to Action*. Washington, DC: The Collaborative Electronic Notebook Systems Association (CENSA), 2000. Available at *www.censa.org/html/Press-Releases/Titanic2020.htm*. Page updated 2000.

MacCarn, Dave, and Thom Shepard. *The Universal Preservation Format*. Boston, MA: WGBH Educational Foundation, 1998. Available at *info.wgbh.org/upf/*.

MacDonald, David. "The Electronic Freedom of Information Act Amendments: A Minor Upgrade to Public Access Law." *Rutgers Computer and Technology Law Journal* 23 (1997), 357–389.

Macklin, Lisa L., and Sarah L. Lockmiller. *Digital Imaging of Photographs: A Practical Approach to Workflow Design and Project Management.* Chicago: American Library Association, 1999.

MacNeil, Heather. "Metadata Strategies and Archival Description: Comparing Apples to Oranges." *Archivaria* 39 (Spring 1995), 22–31.

Mallinson, John C. "Preserving Machine-Readable Archival Records for the Millennia." *Archivaria* 22 (Summer 1986), 147–152.

_____. "On the Preservation of Human and Machine-Readable Records." *Information Technologies and Libraries* 7 (March 1988), 19–22.

Manes, Stephen. "Time and Technology Threaten Digital Archives." *New York Times,* April 7, 1998, sec. F, p. 4, col. 1.

Marker, Hans-Jørgen. "Data Conservation at a Traditional Data Archive." In *History and Electronic Artefacts,* edited by Edward Higgs. Oxford: Clarendon Press, Oxford University Press, 1998, 294–303.

Marsden, Paul. "When Is the Future? Comparative Notes on the Electronic Record-Keeping Projects of the University of Pittsburgh and the University of British Columbia." *Archivaria* 43 (Spring 1997), 158–173.

Mason, Pamela R. "Imaging System Components and Standards." In *Digital Imaging Technology for Preservation: Proceedings from an RLG Symposium Held March 17 and 18, 1994, Cornell University, Ithaca, New York,* edited by Nancy E. Elkington. Mountain View, CA: Research Libraries Group, 1994, 25–40.

Mbambo, Buhle. "Virtual Libraries in Africa: A Dream, or a Knight in Shining Armour?" *IFLA Journal* 22(1996), 229–232.

McCarthy, Gavan. "Records Disposal in the Modern Environment." *Archives and Manuscripts* 18:1 (May 1990), 39–51.

McCarthy, Gavan, and Tim Sherratt. "Mapping Scientific Memory: Understanding the Role of Recordkeeping in Scientific Practice." *Archives and Manuscripts* 24:1 (August 1996), 78–85.

McClure, Charles R., and J. Timothy Spreh. *Analysis and Development of Model Quality Guidelines for Electronic Records Management on State and Federal Websites.* Available at *istweb.syr.edu/~mcclure/nhprc/nhprc_title.html.* Page updated January 1998.

McDonald, John. "Managing Information in an Office Systems Environment: The IMOSA Project. *American Archivist* 58:2 (Spring 1995), 142–153.

_____. "Managing Records in the Modern Office: Taming the Wild Frontier." *Archivaria* 39 (Spring 1995), 70–79.

McKemmish, Sue, and Frank Upward. *Archival Documents.* Melbourne, Australia: Ancora Press, 1993.

Menkus, Belden. "Defining Electronic Records Management." *Records Management Quarterly* 30:1 (January 1996), 38–42.

Messenger, Joel C. "Document Delivery on the Web." *Inform* 13:2 (February 1999), 12–14.

Michelson, Avra. "Description and Reference in the Age of Automation." *American Archivist* 50:2 (Spring 1987), 192–208.

Michelson, Avra, and Jeff Rothenberg. "Scholarly Communication and Information Technology: Exploring the Impact of Changes in the Research Process on Archives." *American Archivist* 55:2 (Spring 1992), 236–315.

Middleton, Martha. "A Discovery: There May be Gold in E-Mail." *National Law Journal* 16:3 (September 20, 1993), 1ff.

Miller, Michael L. "Is the Past Prologue? Appraisal and the New Technologies." In *Archival Management of Electronic Records*, edited by David Bearman. Pittsburgh, PA: Archives and Museum Informatics, 1991, 38–49.

_____. "Disc Players, the Records Manager/Archivist, and the Development of Optical Imaging Applications." *American Archivist* 58:2 (Spring 1995), 170–181.

Mitchell, William J. "Architectural Archives in the Digital Era." *American Archivist* 59:2 (Spring 1996), 200–204.

Mohlhenrich, Janice, ed. *Preservation of Electronic Formats and Electronic Formats for Preservation*. Fort Atkinson, WI: Highsmith, 1993.

Moiseenko, Tatyana. "The Russian Archive System under Pressure in the Information Age." In *History and Electronic Artefacts*, edited by Edward Higgs. Oxford: Clarendon Press, Oxford University Press, 1998, 277–293.

Montana, John. "Legal Issues in EDI." *Records Management Quarterly* 30: 3 (July 1996), 39–45.

Moore, Reagan, Chaitan Baru, Arcot Rajasekar, Bertram Ludaescher, Richard Marciano, Michael Wan, Wayne Schroeder, and Amarnath Gupta. "Collection-Based Persistent Digital Archives: Part 1." *D-Lib Magazine* 6:3 (March 2000). Available at *www.dlib.org/dlib/march00/moore/03moore-pt1.html*. Page updated March 2000.

Morelli, Jeffrey D. "Defining Electronic Records: Problems of Terminology." In *History and Electronic Artefacts*, edited by Edward Higgs. Oxford: Clarendon Press, Oxford University Press, 1998, 169–183.

Morgan, Owen J., and Miranda Welch. "Protecting Confidential Computer Records against Careless Loss." *Records Management Quarterly* 29:3 (July 1995), 16–20.

Mori, Akio. "The Toshiba Business Information Center Moves toward the Virtual Library." *Special Libraries* 85:4 (Fall 1994), 277–280.

Morris, R. J. "Electronic Documents and the History of the late Twentieth Century: Black Holes or Warehouses?" In *History and Electronic Artefacts*, edited by Edward Higgs. Oxford: Clarendon Press, Oxford University Press, 1998, 31–48.

Motz, Arlene. "Applying Records Management Principles to Magnetic Media." *Records Management Quarterly* 20:2 (April 1986), 22–26.

Myburgh, Susan. "Metadata and Its Meaning for Records Managers." *Records and Information Management Report* 14:5 (May 1998), 1–14.

_____. "Information Systems and Records Management." *Records and Information Management Report* 15:2 (February 1999), 1–12.

National Academy of Public Administration. *The Effects of Electronic Recordkeeping on the Historical Record of the U.S. Government: A Report for the National Archives and Records Administration.* Washington, DC: National Academy of Public Administration, 1989.

National Archives and Records Administration. *Managing Electronic Records.* Washington, DC: National Archives and Records Administration, 1990.

_____. *NARA Guidelines for Digitizing Archival Materials for Electronic Access.* Washington, DC: National Archives and Records Administration, 1999. Available at *www.nara.gov/nara/vision/eap/eapspec.html*. Page updated 2000.

National Archives of Canada. *Electronic Records Management Initiatives in the Government of Canada—A Directory.* Available at *www.archives.ca/exec/naweb.dll?fs&0603&e&top&0*. Page updated 1995.

_____. *Electronic Work Environment (EWE)—Vision.* Available at *www.archives.ca/exec/naweb.dll?fs&0603&e&top&0*. Page updated 1995.

_____. *E-Mail Policies in the Government of Canada—A Directory.* Available at *www.archives.ca/exec/naweb.dll?fs&0603&e&top&0*. Page updated 1995.

_____. *Managing Electronic Records in an Electronic Work Environment.* Available at *www.archives.ca/exec/naweb.dll?fs&0603&e&top&0*. Page updated 1995.

_____. *Recordkeeping in the Electronic Work Environment—Vision.* Available at *www.archives.ca/exec/naweb.dll?fs&0603&e&top&0*. Page updated 1995.

National Conference of Commissioners on Uniform State Laws. "Uniform Electronic Transactions Act." Chicago, IL: National Conference of Commissioners on Uniform State Laws, 1999. Available at *www.law.upenn.edu/bll/ulc/uecicta/uetast84.htm*. Page updated July 1999.

National Historical Publications and Records Commission. *Research Issues in Electronic Records*. St. Paul, MN: Minnesota Historical Society, 1991.

National Institute of Standards and Technology. *Database Language SQL*. Federal Information Processing Standards Publication 127–2. Washington, DC: National Institute of Standards and Technology, 1993. Available at *www.itl.nist.gov/fipspubs/fip127-2.htm*. Page updated June 3, 1993.

National Research Council. *Preservation of Historical Records*. Washington, DC: National Academy Press, 1986.

_____. *Preserving Scientific Data on Our Physical Universe: A New Strategy for Archiving the Nation's Scientific Information Resources*. Washington, DC: National Academy Press, 1995.

_____. *Study on the Long-Term Retention of Selected Scientific and Technical Records of the Federal Government: Working Papers*. Washington, DC: National Academy Press, 1995.

Naugler, Harold. *The Archival Appraisal of Machine-Readable Records: A RAMP Study with Guidelines*. Paris, France: UNESCO, 1984.

Neavill, Gordon B. "Electronic Publishing, Libraries, and the Survival of Information." *Library Resources and Technical Services* 28 (January 1984), 76–89.

Nelson, Michael. "Records in the Modern Workplace: Management Concerns." *Archivaria* 39 (Spring 1995), 80–87.

New York Times Magazine. Special Issue, *New York Times* Section 6 (December 5, 1999).

Nicholson, Leslie J. "The Post-Y2K Bug: Technical Obsolescence." *Philadelphia Inquirer,* September 30, 1999.

Northeast Document Conservation Center. *Preservation of Library and Archival Materials: A Manual,* 3rd ed. Andover, MA: Northeast Document Conservation Center, 1999. Also available at *www.nedcc.org/plam3/manhome.htm*. Page updated Feb. 1999.

Norton, Peter, and John Goodman. *Peter Norton's Inside the PC,* 8th ed. Indianapolis: Sams Publishing, Macmillan, 1999.

Nowicke, Carole Elizabeth. "Managing Tomorrow's Records Today: An Experiment in Archival Preservation of Electronic Mail." *Midwestern Archivist* 13:2 (1988), 67–76.

Ohio. "Digital Document Imaging Guidelines for State Agencies in Ohio." Available at *www.ohiojunction.net/erc/imaging/imagingguidelines.html*. Page updated February 22, 2000.

_____. "Managing Electronic Mail: Guidelines for State of Ohio Executive Agencies." Available at *www.ohiojunction.net/erc/email/emailguidelines.html*. Page updated February 22, 2000.

Olson, David. "'Camp Pitt' and the Continuing Education of Government Archivists, 1989–1996." *American Archivist* 60:2 (Spring 1997), 202–215.

Oppenheim, C. "Virtual Reality and the Virtual Library." *Information Services and Use* 13:3 (1993), 215–227.

Orr, John P., Jr. "Records Retention for ADP Systems." *CPA Journal* 62 (October 1992), 67–68.

O'Rourke, Tony. "Chadwyck-Healey—Electronic Resources for the Virtual Library: A Publisher's Perspective of Preservation and Access." *Publications of Essen University Library* 20 (1996), 160–169.

O'Shea, Greg, and David Roberts. "Living in a Digital World: Reorganizing the Electronic and Post-Custodial Realities." *Archives and Manuscripts* 24:2 (November 1996), 286–311.

Ostrow, Stephen E. *Digitizing Historical Pictorial Collections for the Internet.* Washington, DC: Council on Library and Information Resources, 1998.

O'Toole, James M. "On the Idea of Permanence." *American Archivist* 52:1 (1989), 10–25.

Parer, Dagmar, and Keith Parrott. "Management Practices in the Electronic Records Environment." *Archives and Manuscripts* 22:1 (May 1994), 106–122.

Pasterczyk, Catherine E. "Federal E-Mail Management: A Records Manager's View of *Armstrong v. Executive Office of the President.*" *Records Management Quarterly* 32:2 (1998), 10–22.

Paton, Christopher Ann. "Annotated Selected Bibliography of Works Relating to Sound Recordings and Magnetic and Optical Media." *Midwestern Archivist* 16:1 (1991), 31–48.

_____. "Preservation Re-Recording of Audio Recordings in Archives: Problems, Priorities, Technologies, and Recommendations. *American Archivist* 61:1 (Spring 1998), 188–219.

Perritt, Henry H., Jr. "Electronic Records Management and Archives." *University of Pittsburgh Law Review* (Summer 1992), 963–1024.

_____. "Electronic Freedom of Information." *Administrative Law Review* 50:2 (1998), 391–419.

Peterson, Trudy Huskamp. "Archival Principles and Records of the New Technology." *American Archivist* 47:4 (Fall 1984), 383–393.

Petherbridge, Guy, ed. *Conservation of Library and Archive Materials and the Graphic Arts.* London: Butterworths, 1987.

Phillips, John T. "Electronic Junk Mail." *Records Management Quarterly* 26:3 (July 1992), 38–41, 52.

_____. "Virtual Records and Virtual Archives." *Records Management Quarterly* 28:1 (January 1994), 42–45, 60.

_____. "Metadata: Information About Electronic Records." *Records Management Quarterly* 29:4 (October 1995), 52–55, 73.

_____. "Do Electronic Records Create Business Risk?" *Records Management Quarterly* 31:1 (January 1997), 40–42.

_____. "What's in That Data Warehouse?" *Records Management Quarterly* 31:2 (April 1997), 54–56.

Phillips, Margaret E. "The National Library of Australia: Ensuring Long-Term Access to Online Publications." *Journal of Electronic Publishing* 4:4 (June 1999). Available at *www.press.umich.edu/jep/04–04/phillips.html*. Page updated June 1999.

Piasecki, Sara J. "Legal Admissibility of Electronic Records as Evidence and Implications for Records Management." *American Archivist* 58:1 (Winter 1995), 54–64.

Piche, Jean-Stephan. "Doing What's Possible with What We've Got: Using the World Wide Web to Integrate Archival Functions." *American Archivist* 61:1 (Spring 1998), 106–123.

Piggott, Sylvia E. A. "The Virtual Library: Almost There." *Special Libraries* 84:4 (1993), 206–212.

Polito, Jessica. "A Primer on Public-Key Cryptography." *Journal of Electronic Publishing* 4:4 (June 1999). Available at *www.press.umich.edu/jep/04-04/polito.html*. Page updated June 1999.

Poole, Frazer G. "Some Aspects of the Conservation Problem in Archives." *American Archivist* 40:2 (April 1977), 163–171.

Powell, Alan. "Management Models and Measurement in the Virtual Library." *Special Libraries* 85:4 (Fall 1994), 260–263.

Preservation. Special Issue of *American Archivist* 53:2 (Spring 1990), 184–369.

Preservation of Archival Materials: A Report of the Task Force on Archival Selection to the Commission on Preservation and Access. Washington, DC: Commission on Preservation and Access, 1993.

Prochaska, Alice. "Special Collections in the British Library and Electronic Media." In *History and Electronic Artefacts*, edited by Edward Higgs. Oxford: Clarendon Press, Oxford University Press, 1998, 243–252.

Public Records Office Victoria (Australia). *Victorian Electronic Records Strategy Final Report.* Victoria: Public Records Office Victoria, 1998. Available at *www.prov.vic.gov.au/VERS/*.

Pursell, Carroll. "Preservation Technologies: As Answers Get Easier, Questions Remain Hard." *Public Historian* 13:3 (Summer 1991), 113–116.

Rayward, W. Boyd. "Electronic Information and the Functional Integration of Libraries, Museums, and Archives." In *History and Electronic Artefacts*, edited by Edward Higgs. Oxford: Clarendon Press, Oxford University Press, 1998, 207–226.

Reed, Barbara. "Metadata: Core Record or Core Business?" *Archives and Manuscripts* 25:2 (November 1997), 218–241.

Reid, Lydia J. E. "Electronic Records Training: Suggestions for the Implementation of the CART Curriculum." *American Archivist* 58:3 (Summer 1995), 326–341.

Reinitzer, Sigrid. "The Function of a Traditional Library as a Virtual Library: A Comparison." *Publications of Essen University Library* 18 (1995), 361–368.

Renehan, Marion. "Unassailable Evidence: The Nexus between Recordkeeping and Public Sector Accountability." *Archives and Manuscripts* 21:1 (May 1993), 62–76.

Rhodes, Steven B. "Archival and Records Management Automation." *Records Management Quarterly* 25:2 (April 1991), 12–17.

Ritzenthaler, Mary Lynn. *Archives and Manuscripts: Conservation.* Chicago: Society of American Archivists, 1983.

_____. *Preserving Archives and Manuscripts.* Chicago: Society of American Archivists, 1993.

Roberts, David. "Defining Electronic Records, Documents and Data." *Archives and Manuscripts* 22:1 (May 1994), 14–26.

Ross, Seamus. "The Expanding World of Electronic Information and the Past's Future." In *History and Electronic Artefacts*, edited by Edward Higgs. Oxford: Clarendon Press, Oxford University Press, 1998, 5–28.

Rothenberg, Jeff. "Ensuring the Longevity of Digital Documents." *Scientific American* 272:1 (January 1995), 42–47.

_____. *Avoiding Technological Quicksand: Finding a Viable Technical Foundation for Digital Preservation.* Washington, DC: Council on Library and Information Resources, 1999.

Rowley, Jennifer. "Libraries and the Electronic Information Marketplace." *Library Review* 45:7 (1996), 6–18.

Saffady, William. "Stability, Care, and Handling of Microforms, Magnetic Media and Optical Disks." *Library Technology Reports* 27:1 (1991), 5–116.

_____. *Electronic Document Imaging Systems: Design, Evaluation, and Implementation.* Westport, CT: Meckler, 1993.

_____. *Knowledge Management: A Manager's Briefing.* Prairie Village, KS: Association of Records Managers and Administrators, 1998.

_____. *Managing Electronic Records,* 2nd ed. Prairie Village, KS: ARMA International, 1998.

Samuel, Jean. "Electronic Mail: Information Exchange or Information Loss?" In *History and Electronic Artefacts*, edited by Edward Higgs. Oxford: Clarendon Press, Oxford University Press, 1998, 101–119.

Sanders, Terry. *Into the Future: On the Preservation of Knowledge in the Electronic Age.* Video/film. Santa Monica, CA: American Film Foundation, 1997.

Saunders, Laverna M. "The Virtual Library Revisited." *Computers in Libraries* 12:10 (1992), 51–54.

Schellenberg, T. R. "Appraisal of Modern Public Records." In *A Modern Archives Reader*, edited by Maygene F. Daniels and Timothy Walch. Washington, DC: National Archives and Records Service, 1984.

Schurer, Kevin. "The Implications of Information Technology for the Future Study of History." In *History and Electronic Artefacts*, edited by Edward Higgs. Oxford: Clarendon Press, Oxford University Press, 1998, 155–168.

Schwarz, Annette Winkel. "The Virtual Catalogue, the Virtual Library, and the Virtual Librarian." *The LIBER Quarterly* 5 (1995), 361–372.

Scott, Mary W. "Digital Imagery: Here Today, but What About Tomorrow?" *Proceedings of the Geoscience Information Society, October 26–29, 1992, 1–4.*

Seiler, Laren H. "The Concept of the Book in the Age of Digital Electronic Medium." *Library Software Review* 11:1 (January-February 1992), 19–29.

Sever, Shmuel, and Cecilia H. Harel. "Managing the Virtual Library: Issues and Challenges." *Publications of the Essen University Library* 18 (1995), 369–382.

Shahani, Chandru J., and William K. Wilson. "Preservation of Libraries and Archives." *American Scientist* 75 (May/June 1987), 240–251.

Simpson, Helen. "The Management of Electronic Information Resources in a Corporate Environment." In *History and Electronic Artefacts*, edited by Edward Higgs. Oxford: Clarendon Press, Oxford University Press, 1998, 87–100.

Skupsky, Donald S. "Establishing Retention Periods for Electronic Records." *Records Management Quarterly* 27:2 (April 1993), 40–43, 49.

_____. "The Law of Electronic Mail: The Impact of the White House Case on You." *Records Management Quarterly* 28:1(January 1994), 32, 36–37, 40.

Smith, Abby. "Digitization Prompts New Preservation-and-Access Strategies." *CLIR Issues* 1 (January/February 1998), 1, 7.

_____. "Preservation in the Future Tense." *CLIR Issues* 3 (May/June 1998).

_____. "The Hybrid Model of Preservation Reformatting." *CLIR Issues* 6 (November/December 1998), 2, 4.

_____. *Why Digitize?* Washington, DC: Council on Library and Information Resources, 1999. Available at *www.clir.org/cpa/reports/pub80-smith/pub80.html*. Page updated February 1999.

Smith, Clive D. "Implementation of Imaging Technology for Record-keeping at the World Bank." *Bulletin of the American Society for Information Science* 23:5 (June/July 1997), 25–29.

Smith, Steve. "Sources for Digital Imaging Projects." *Abbey Newsletter* 22:2 (1998), 22–23.

Smither, Roger. "Formats and Standards: A Film Archive Perspective on Exchanging Computerized Data." *American Archivist* 50:3 (Summer 1987), 324–337.

Society of American Archivists. "Archival Issues Raised by Information Stored in Electronic Form." Chicago, IL: Society of American Archivists, no date.

Sorokin, Leo T. "The Computerization of Government Information: Does it Circumvent Public Access under the Freedom of Information Act and the Depository Library Program?" *Columbia Journal of Law & Social Problems* (1991), 267–298.

Sprehe, J. Timothy. "Archiving Electronic Databases: The NAPA National Academy of Public Administration Report." *Inform* 6:3 (March 1992), 28–31.

Stahl, D. Gail. "The Virtual Library: Prospect and Promise." *Special Libraries* 84:4 (1993), 202–205.

Standards Australia. *Records Management.* Australian Standard 4390. Homebush, NSW: Standards Association of Australia, 1996.

Stanford University. *Conservation On-Line (CoOL).* Available at *palimpsest.stanford.edu/.* Page updated April 20, 2000.

State University of New York at Albany, Center for Technology in Government. *Models for Action: Practical Approaches to Electronic Records Management and Preservation.* Available at *www.ctg.albany.edu/resources/pdfrpwp/mfa.pdf.*

_____. *Practical Tools for Electronic Records Management and Preservation.* Available at *www.ctg.albany.edu/resources/abstract/mfa_toolkit.html.* Page updated June 29, 1999.

Stephens, David O. "Megatrends in Records Management." *Records Management Quarterly* 32:1 (January 1998), 3–9.

Stephens, David O., and Roderick C. Wallace. *Electronic Records Retention: An Introduction.* Prairie Village, KS: ARMA International, 1997.

Stewart, Eleanor. "Why Library Preservation Should Plan for a Digital Future." *Abbey Newsletter* 22:3 (1998), 33, 36–38.

Stielow, Frederick J. "Archival Theory and the Preservation of Electronic Media: Opportunities and Standards below the Cutting Edge." *American Archivist* 55:2 (Spring 1992), 332–342.

_____. "The Impact of Information Technology on Archival Theory: A Discourse on the Automation Pedagogy." *Journal for Education in Library and Information Science* 34:1 (Winter 1993), 48–65.

Stout, Lee. "The Role of University Archives in the Campus Information Environment." *American Archivist* 58:2 (Spring 1995), 124–141.

Swade, Doron. "Preserving Software in an Object-Centered Culture." In *History and Electronic Artefacts*, edited by Edward Higgs. Oxford: Clarendon Press, Oxford University Press, 1998, 195–206.

Tankersley, Michael E. "How the Electronic Freedom of Information Act Amendments of 1996 Update Access for the Information Age." *Administrative Law Review* 50:2 (1998), 421–458.

Taylor, Hugh. "Information Ecology and the Archives in the 1980s." *Archivaria* 18 (Summer 1984), 25–37.

_____. "Transformation in the Archives: Technological Adjustment or Paradigm Shift?" *Archivaria* 25 (Winter 1987/88), 12–28.

_____. "'My Very Act and Deed:' Some Reflections on the Role of Textual Records in the Conduct of Affairs." *American Archivist* 51:4 (Fall 1988), 456–469.

Thibodeau, Kenneth. "To Be or Not To Be: Archives for Electronic Records." In *Archival Management of Electronic Records*, edited by David Bearman. Pittsburgh, PA: Archives and Museum Informatics, 1991, 1–13.

To Scan or Not To Scan: What Are the Questions? Proceedings of a SOLINET Conference on Digitizing Projects for Libraries and Archives, May 2, 1996. Atlanta, GA: SOLINET, 1997.

Turnbaugh, Roy. "Information Technology, Records, and State Archives." *American Archivist* 60:2 (Spring 1997), 184–201.

Understanding Computers: Memory and Storage. Alexandria, VA: Time-Life, 1990.

United Nations Advisory Committee for the Coordination of Information Systems (ACCIS). *Management of Electronic Records: Issues and Guidelines*. New York: United Nations, 1990.

_____. *Strategic Issues for Electronic Records Management: Toward Open System Interconnection*. New York: United Nations, 1992.

_____. *Optical Storage: An Overview of the Technology and Its Use within the United Nations System*. New York: United Nations, 1993.

United States Congress, House Committee on Government Operations. *Taking a Byte out of History: The Archival Preservation of Federal Computer Records*. House Report 101-987. Washington, DC: House of Representatives, 1990.

University of British Columbia. *The Preservation of the Integrity of Electronic Records*. Available at *www.slais.ubc.ca/users/duranti/intro.htm*. Page updated 1997.

University of Pittsburgh. *Functional Requirements for Evidence in Recordkeeping*. Available at *www.sis.pitt.edu/~nhprc/meta96.html*. Page updated 1998.

University of West Florida. "Policy on Electronic Mail." Available at *nautical.uwf.edu/org/*.

Upward, Frank. "Structuring the Records Continuum, Part One: Post-Custodial Principles and Properties." *Archives and Manuscripts* 24:2 (November 1996), 268–285.

———. "Structuring the Records Continuum, Part Two: Structuration Theory and Recordkeeping." *Archives and Manuscripts* 25:1 (February 1997), 14–35.

Upward, Frank, and Sue McKemmish. "Somewhere Beyond Custody." *Archives and Manuscripts* 22:1 (May 1994), 136–149.

Van Bogart, John W. C. *Magnetic Tape Storage and Handling: A Guide for Libraries and Archives.* Washington, DC: Commission on Preservation and Access; St. Paul, MN: National Media Laboratory, 1995.

Varon, Elana. "Storage Dilemma Looms." *Federal Computer Week,* January 25, 1999. Available at *www.fcw.com/pubs/fcw/1999/0125/ fcw-newsstorage-1-25-99.html*.

Waegemann, C. Peter. "Preservation of Information." *Records and Retrieval Report* 2:3 (March 1986), 1–15.

Walch, Victoria Irons. "Checklist of Standards Applicable to the Preservation of Archives and Manuscripts." *American Archivist* 53:2 (Spring 1990), 324–338.

Walker, Frank L. and George R. Thoma. "Access Techniques for Document Image Databases." *Library Trends* 38:4 (Spring 1990), 751–786.

Walker, Gay. "Storing Paper." *Records and Retrieval Report* 3:7 (September 1987), 1–12.

———. "Advanced Preservation Planning at Yale." *Microform Review* 18 (Winter 1989), 20–28.

Wallace, David. "Metadata and Archival Management of Electronic Records: A Review." *Archivaria* 36 (Autumn 1993), 87–110.

———. "Managing the Present: Metadata as Archival Description." *Archivaria* 39 (Spring 1995), 11–21.

Wallot, Jean-Pierre. "Archival Oneness in the Midst of Diversity." *American Archivist* 57:2 (Spring 1994).

Walters, Tyler O. "Thinking about Archival Preservation in the '90s and Beyond: Some Recent Publications and Their Implications for Archivists." *American Archivist* 58:4 (Fall 1995), 476–492.

———. "Contemporary Archival Appraisal Methods and Preservation Decision-Making." *American Archivist* 59:3 (Summer 1996), 322–339.

Walters, Tyler O., in association with Ivan E. Hanthorn. "Special Collections Repositories at Association of Research Libraries Institutions: A Study of Current Practices in Preservation Management." *American Archivist* 61:1 (Spring 1998), 158–187.

Ward, Scott W., and Brian A. Cole. "Selecting Record Media." *Records Management Quarterly* 29:3 (July 1995), 3–6.

Waters, Donald J. *From Microfilm to Digital Imagery: On the Feasibility of a Project to Study the Means, Costs and Benefits of Converting Large Quantities of Preserved Library Materials from Microfilm to Digital Images*. Washington, DC: Commission on Preservation and Access, 1991.

_____. *Electronic Technologies and Preservation*. Washington, DC: Commission on Preservation and Access, 1992.

_____. "Transforming Libraries through Digital Preservation." In *Digital Imaging Technology for Preservation: Proceedings from an RLG Symposium Held March 17 and 18, 1994, Cornell University, Ithaca, New York*, edited by Nancy E. Elkington. Mountain View, CA: Research Libraries Group, 1994, 115–127.

_____. "What Are Digital Libraries?" *CLIR Issues* 4 (July/August 1998), 1, 6–7.

_____. "Digital Preservation?" *CLIR Issues* 6 (November/December 1998), 1, 5–6.

Waters, Donald J., and Shari Weaver. *The Organizational Phase of Project Open Book*. Washington, DC: Commission on Preservation and Access, 1992.

Watson, Andrea, and P. Toby Graham. "*CSS Alabama* Digital Collection: A Special Collections Digitization Project." *American Archivist* 61:1 (Spring 1998), 124–135.

Weaver, Shari L. "Quality Control." In *Digital Imaging Technology for Preservation: Proceedings from an RLG Symposium Held March 17 and 18, 1994, Cornell University, Ithaca, New York*, edited by Nancy E. Elkington. Mountain View, CA: Research Libraries Group, 1994, 81–98.

Weber, Hartmut, and Marianne Orr. *Digitization as a Method of Preservation?* Washington, DC: Council on Library and Information Resources, 1997.

Weber, Lisa B. *Electronic Records Issues: A Report to the Commission*. Washington, DC: National Historical Publications and Records Commission, 1990.

_____. "Electronic Records: Too Ephemeral?" *Inform* 6:2 (February 1992), 32–36.

Weiner, Robert G. "The Virtual Library and Its Implications." *Public and Access Services Quarterly* 2:1 (1996), 41–45.

Wettengel, Michael. "German Unification and Electronic Records." In *History and Electronic Artefacts*, edited by Edward Higgs. Oxford: Clarendon Press, Oxford University Press, 1998, 265–276.

Wheaton, Bruce R. "A Computer Database System to Store and Display Archival Data on Correspondence of Historical Significance." *American Archivist* 45:4 (Fall 1982), 455–466.

White, Ron. *How Computers Work*. Emeryville, CA: Ziff-Davis, 1997.

Wiederhold, Gio. "Digital Libraries: Value and Productivity." *Communications of the ACM* 38:4 (1995), 85–96.

Wilhelm, Henry. *The Permanence and Care of Color Photographs: Traditional and Digital Color Print, Color Negatives, Slide, and Motion Pictures*. Grinnel, IA: Preservation Publishing, 1993.

Williams, Don R. "Data Conversion: A Tutorial on Electronic Document Imaging." In *Digital Imaging Technology for Preservation: Proceedings from an RLG Symposium Held March 17 and 18, 1994, Cornell University, Ithaca, New York*, edited by Nancy E. Elkington. Mountain View, CA: The Research Libraries Group, 1994, 50–80.

World Wide Web Consortium (W3C). "Web Characterization Terminology and Definition Sheet." Available at *www.w3c.org/1999/WCA-terms/*.

_____. "Metadata and Resource Description." Available at *www.w3org/Metadata/*.

Yen, David, and Huang-Lian Tang. "Future Trends of Computer-Based Information Systems." *Records Management Quarterly* 22:4 (October 1988), 12–19.

Zhao, Dian G., and Anne Ramsden. "Report on the ELINOR Electronic Library Pilot." *Information Services and Use* 15 (1995), 199–212.

Zweig, Ronald W. "Electronic Fingerprints and the Use of Documents." In *History and Electronic Artefacts*, edited by Edward Higgs. Oxford: Clarendon Press, Oxford University Press, 1998, 49–58.

INDEX